Quick Guide

GAZEBOS

CREATIVE HOMEOWNER PRESS®

COPYRIGHT © 1995
CREATIVE HOMEOWNER PRESS®
A Division of Federal Marketing Corp.
Upper Saddle River, NJ

Quick Guide is a registered trademark of Creative Homeowner Press®

Manufactured in the United States of America

Writers: Drew Corinchock
         James Russell
         David Schiff
         Joseph F. Wajszczuk Jr.
Editor: David Schiff
Associate Editor: Alexander Samuelson
Copy Editor: Candace B. Levy, Ph.D.

Art Director: Annie Jeon
Graphic Designer: Fernando Colon Jr.
Illustrators: Jim Randolph
              Paul M. Schumm

Cover Design: Warren Ramezzana
Cover Illustrations: Paul M. Schumm

Electronic Prepress: TBC Color Imaging, Inc.
Printed at: Quebecor Printing Inc.

Current Printing (last digit)
10 9 8 7 6 5 4 3 2 1

Quick Guide: Gazebos
Library of Congress Catalog Card Number: 95-70916
ISBN: 1-880029-52-9 (paper)

CREATIVE HOMEOWNER PRESS®
A Division of Federal Marketing Corp.
24 Park Way
Upper Saddle River, NJ 07458

C O N T E N T S

SAFETY FIRST

Though all the designs and methods in this book have been tested for safety, it is not possible to overstate the importance of using the safest construction methods possible. What follows are reminders; some do's and don'ts of basic carpentry. They are not substitutes for your own common sense.

- *Always* use caution, care, and good judgment when following the procedures described in this book.

- *Always* be sure that the electrical setup is safe; be sure that no circuit is overloaded, and that all power tools and electrical outlets are properly grounded. Do not use power tools in wet locations.

- *Always* read container labels on paints, solvents, and other products; provide ventilation, and observe all other warnings.

- *Always* read the tool manufacturer's instructions for using a tool, especially the warnings.

- *Always* use holders or pushers to work pieces shorter than 3 inches on a table saw or jointer. Avoid working short pieces if you can.

- *Always* remove the key from any drill chuck (portable or press) before starting the drill.

- *Always* pay deliberate attention to how a tool works so that you can avoid being injured.

- *Always* know the limitations of your tools. Do not try to force them to do what they were not designed to do.

- *Always* make sure that any adjustment is locked before proceeding. For example, always check the rip fence on a table saw or the bevel adjustment on a portable saw before starting to work.

- *Always* clamp small pieces firmly to a bench or other work surfaces when sawing or drilling.

- *Always* wear the appropriate rubber or work gloves when handling chemicals, heavy construction or when sanding.

- *Always* wear a disposable mask when working with odors, dusts or mists. Use a special respirator when working with toxic substances.

- *Always* wear eye protection, especially when using power tools or striking metal on metal or concrete; a chip can fly off, for example, when chiseling concrete.

- *Always* be aware that there is never time for your body's reflexes to save you from injury from a power tool in a dangerous situation; everything happens too fast. Be *alert!*

- *Always* keep your hands away from the business ends of blades, cutters and bits.

- *Always* hold a portable circular saw with both hands so that you will know where your hands are.

- *Always* use a drill with an auxiliary handle to control the torque when large size bits are used.

- *Always* check your local building codes when planning new construction. The codes are intended to protect public safety and should be observed to the letter.

- *Never* work with power tools when you are tired or under the influence of alcohol or drugs.

- *Never* cut very small pieces of wood or pipe. Whenever possible, cut small pieces off larger pieces.

- *Never* change a blade or a bit unless the power cord is unplugged. Do not depend on the switch being off; you might accidentally hit it.

- *Never* work in insufficient lighting.

- *Never* work while wearing loose clothing, hanging hair, open cuffs, or jewelry.

- *Never* work with dull tools. Have them sharpened, or learn how to sharpen them yourself.

- *Never* use a power tool on a work piece that is not firmly supported or clamped.

- *Never* saw a work piece that spans a large distance between horses without close support on either side of the kerf; the piece can bend, closing the kerf and jamming the blade, causing saw kickback.

- *Never* support a work piece with your leg or other part of your body when sawing.

- *Never* carry sharp or pointed tools, such as utility knives, awls, or chisels in your pocket. If you want to carry tools, use a special-purpose tool belt with leather pockets and holders.

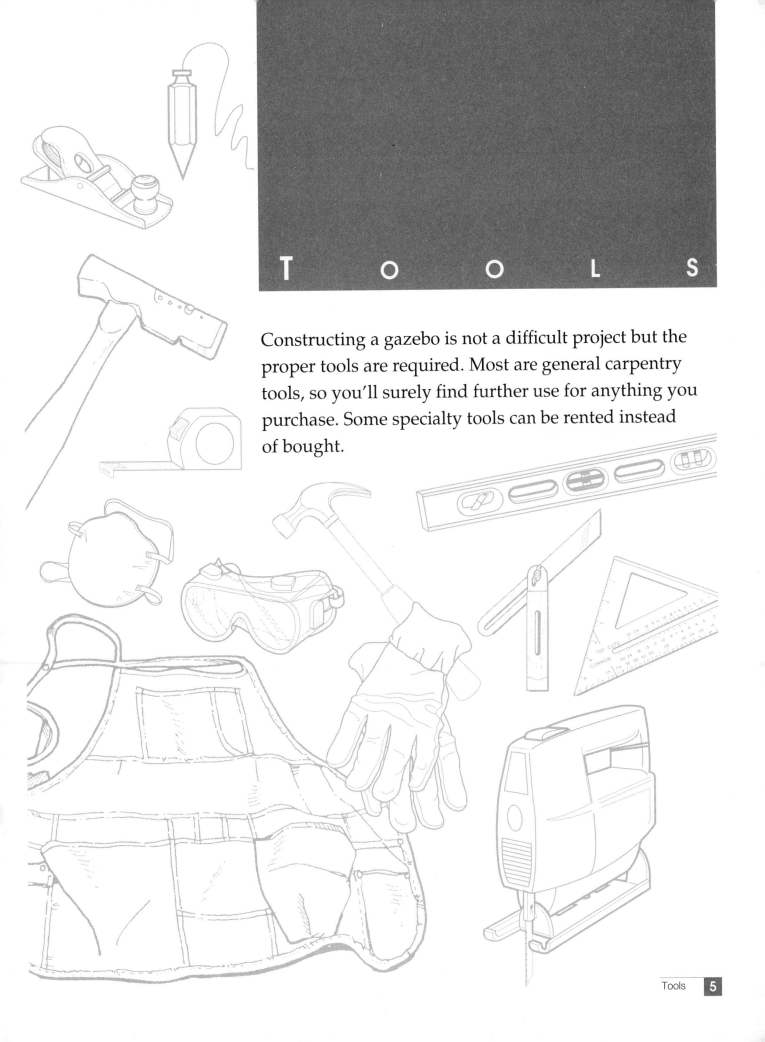

T O O L S

Constructing a gazebo is not a difficult project but the proper tools are required. Most are general carpentry tools, so you'll surely find further use for anything you purchase. Some specialty tools can be rented instead of bought.

What Tools Are Needed?

This chapter should not be read as a wish list. For generations, carpenters—skilled craftsmen—managed quite well with little more than a hammer, a saw, some chisels, and a few planes. Except for the additions of the electric drill and circular saw, your toolbox does not need to include more than that same basic cache. Remember that power tools have been created for convenience—no one purchase will ever be able to replace skill, experience, and a little creativity.

Too many carpenters confuse want with need and end up buying tools that they really have no use for—tools that wind up collecting dust and rust at the bottom of the box.

In most cases, one tool can do another's job just as conveniently; which one you use often depends simply on which one you already own. At other times, you will find that, given a little extra time, it's possible to "make do" with what you have. Carpentry is an exercise in improvisation.

This chapter outlines the basic tools used in the construction of gazebos. The tools fall into three major categories: tools for layout and excavation; cutting tools and joining tools; and everything else.

Purchase the least expensive tool that will meet or exceed all of your criteria and then some. This usually means purchasing the best tool you can afford. (Best does not always mean most expensive, so be sure of what you're buying.) A "bargain" tool will not seem to be that great a bargain if its limitations remind you of that fact every time you pick it up.

One-time jobs can be done very professionally and economically with rented tools. Rental shops deal with professional-caliber tools that will perform better than their less expensive counterparts. Renting is a great opportunity to use a more exotic tool at a fraction of its purchase price.

And should you eventually decide to purchase that particular type of tool, your on-site experience will better enable you to pick out the model that's right for you.

Layout & Excavation Tools

Marking Out the Site

A tape measure is essential for just about any building project. For this type of work, you'll find that a 25- or 30-foot tape will be the most useful for both long and short measurements. Good tape measures will have the first foot divided into 1/32-inch lengths for really precise work. Tapes with a 1-inch-wide blade are a little more bulky than 3/4-inch blades, but the blades are much more rigid and can be extended farther without folding. This really can come in handy for one-person measuring jobs.

A chalkline is nothing more than that—a roll of string held inside a chalk-filled container. It only takes a couple seconds to "snap a line." Stretch the string against a flat surface and pluck it to produce a straight, chalked layout line. Although red chalk may be a little easier to see, stick with blue. The red pigment is permanent and can stain anything it gets in contact with (hands, wood, etc.).

A plumb bob relies on gravity to enable you to drop a perfectly vertical line from a given spot. The heavy pointed bob is suspended on a string and is useful for aligning posts with pinpoint accuracy. Some chalklines can also be used as plumb bobs.

Digging Holes

If you have to sink only a few posts or if you have a really strong back, you can dig holes by hand with a posthole digger. This double-handled tool is designed to cut deep narrow holes and scoop out the dirt with its clamshell-like blades.

For larger projects, you'll thank yourself for renting a power auger to speed up the job. Power augers are powered by a gasoline engine and work just like a giant drill. Some models can be handled by one person, others require two. You will still need a posthole digger to clean out the holes when you're finished with the auger.

Whether you are using the auger or a posthole digger, if you run into rock, you'll need a wrecking bar (also referred to as a breaking bar) to break up the stone or to wedge it loose. Roots can also slow down your progress; cut them out with either a hand ax or branch pruners.

Levels

There are two levels that can assist you in making sure that the longest spans are "on the level": a water level and a line level.

A water level consists of a pair of clear graduated vials fitted onto a long tube (your garden hose will do nicely). Water naturally seeks its

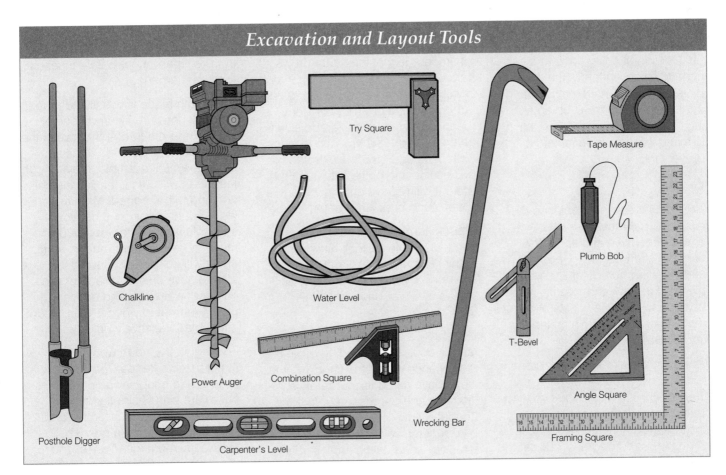

Posthole Digger · Power Auger · Chalkline · Water Level · Combination Square · Try Square · Wrecking Bar · Tape Measure · Plumb Bob · T-Bevel · Angle Square · Framing Square · Carpenter's Level

own level; when the water levels in the two tubes are even, the points are level with each other. This is the most accurate method for measuring over long distances. A line level consists of only a single vial. It's designed to be hooked to a string for leveling long spans. Make sure that the string is taut to ensure an accurate measurement.

The carpenter's level is a workhorse on any construction site. Available in 2-foot and 4-foot lengths, you will use one for leveling beams, ledgers, and making sure posts are plumb. Take special care of your level; all it takes is one good drop to make it inaccurate. One way to test your level is by setting it on top of a level surface. Now flip it over. The bubbles should still be in the center; if they've moved, then your level is off.

A torpedo level is a good tool for plumbing up concrete forms and J-bolts as you set them in wet concrete. Its compact size makes it a handy addition to your toolbox.

Squares

A framing square is made from a single piece of steel or aluminum and is useful for laying out stair stringers and rafters. Its large size makes it good for squaring up large boards and calibrating your other squares, but when you're setting individual tools, such as your circular saw, you will probably find it's more convenient to use a smaller square.

A combination square is adjustable. The body of this square contains both 90- and 45-degree ends and can slide up and down the blade if you unlock the thumbscrew. The moveable body makes this tool ideal for transferring depth measurements or running a line along a board.

Angle squares are thick, strong, triangular castings of either aluminum or plastic that are tough enough to withstand the rigors of general construction without losing their accuracy. The angle square's triangular shape enables you to lay

out a 45-degree angle as quickly as a 90-degree angle. Using markings on the body, it is also possible to lay out angles other than 90 degrees, as when laying out rafters. The edges of this square can also be used as an accurate cutting guide.

Probably the best tool for gauging and transferring angles other than 45 and 90 degrees is a sliding T-bevel (also known as a bevel gauge). A bevel gauge has a flat metal blade that can be locked into a wooden or plastic handle at any angle. A bevel gauge is great for transferring an existing angle on the actual project, it can also be used in conjunction with a protractor to record a specific angle (for example, if you wanted to draw a 25-degree angle).

Cutting & Joining

Most people consider cutting and joining to be the most enjoyable part of carpentry. This feeling and accomplishment is the result of actually working with the wood, cutting and shaping it to fit your design. That feeling of enjoyment will be enhanced if you work with the correct tools. More important, having the right tool for a specific job and knowing how to use it are the best ways to avoid wasting material and to prevent injuries.

Cutting

The circular saw has replaced the handsaw in almost every situation. That's because a circular saw is capable of crosscutting, ripping, and beveling boards or sheets of plywood quickly and cleanly. It can be used to create a variety of common joints, such as miters, laps, and dadoes.

The most popular saws with carpenters and do-it-yourselfers alike are the models that take a 7¼-inch blade. This blade size will enable you to cut to a maximum depth of about 2½ inches at 90 degrees. (Larger saws are available for cutting thicker material, but they're generally too bulky for this type of use.)

Choosing a Circular Saw

There are many options that distinguish one saw from another, the most important of which is its power. Don't judge a saw's performance by its horsepower rating, but by the amount of amperage that the motor draws. Low-cost saws may have only 9- or 10-amp motors with drive shafts and arbors running on rollers or sleeve bearings. A contractor-grade saw is rated at 12 or 13 amps and is made with ball bearings. This extra power will enable it to better withstand the wear it will receive cutting through a lot of tough pressure-treated lumber.

Plastic housings are no longer the mark of an inferior tool; however, a thin, stamped metal foot is. A thin, stamped steel base won't stay as flat as a thicker base that is either extruded or cast.

For safety's sake, be sure that your saw is double insulated, to minimize any chance of electric shock. Some saws have an additional safety switch that must be depressed before the trigger will work. Another feature to look for on a saw is an arbor lock. The lock secures the arbor nut and prevents the blade from turning while you are changing blades.

Choosing a Blade

For general all-purpose use, carbide blades are the best for achieving smooth, precise cuts. Carbide blades may cost a few dollars more than a comparable blade made from high-speed steel, but you can expect it to cut five times longer before it needs to be resharpened.

A 24-tooth blade is usually adequate for deck construction and general use. (There is a trade-off between the number of teeth and cut rates and cut quality. For example, a blade with less teeth will cut faster, but the cuts will tend to be ragged. More teeth will produce a finer cut, but your saw will also have to work harder to move more teeth through the wood, and it will cut slower.) It's a good idea to have an extra blade or two on hand; wet wood and dense pressure-treated wood will dull your saw's blade relatively quickly.

For angle cuts, you'll want to use a motorized miter box. These tools (also called chop saws or cutoff saws) are simply circular saws mounted on a pivot assembly and are designed to make precise crosscuts in boards, planks, and pieces of trim. Chop saws are more expensive than circular saws, but they make it possible to cut difficult angles precisely and quickly.

A saber saw is a good choice for cutting decorative curves on the ends of rafters and for making elaborate pieces of trim. A saber saw can cut

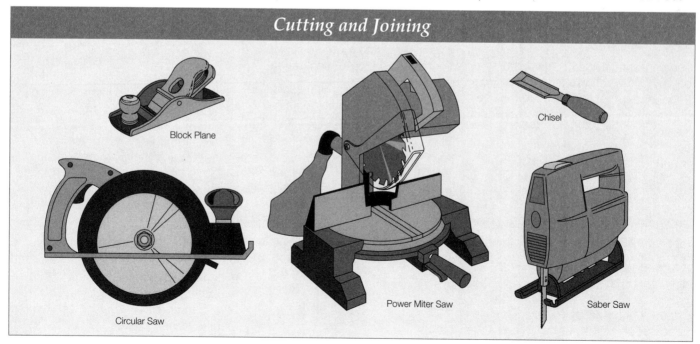

Cutting and Joining

Block Plane

Chisel

Circular Saw

Power Miter Saw

Saber Saw

curves, make cutouts, and finish cuts started by a circular saw.

For certain types of cuts, nothing will completely replace a good handsaw. A handsaw is just the thing whenever you have just a few cuts to do, for those spots where a circular saw can't reach, or when you want to finish off a circular saw cut. A 15-inch saw with 10 to 12 teeth per inch (tpi) will cut well and still fit into your toolbox.

Joinery Tools

No matter how adept you become with your power tools, sooner or later you will end up falling back on certain old reliables to achieve close-fitting joints. A block plane is great to carry along with you on the site. A properly set plane will trim a shaving off at a time, until the joint matches up perfectly. A plane is also handy for softening hard edges that might splinter or catch someone's clothing.

A set of three chisels, 3/4 inch, 1 inch, and 1½ inches, will also be useful for close paring. The blades must be kept as sharp as possible for these tools to work safely and smoothly. Pressure-treated wood will dull steel edges more quickly than other types of wood.

Other Required Construction Tools

There are a few tools that don't really fit into one specific category or that seem to apply to more than one category, and for that reason, they warrant their own special mention.

For every project in this book, it is assumed that you have an electric drill. (If you don't, you should pick up one with a 3/8-inch chuck, variable speed control, and a reverse switch.) Make sure that your drill is sufficiently powered (at least 3 amps) to handle the kind of abuse that it will receive on the job. You will discover that by inserting the proper bit in the chuck, your drill is also able to drive screws faster than you could ever do by hand.

Common sense should tell you not to do carpentry without first having some basic safety equipment, such as eye and ear protection.

Wear safety goggles or plastic glasses whenever you are working with power tools or chemicals…period. Make sure your eye protection conforms to American National Standards Institute (ANSI) Z87.1 or Canadian Standards Association (CSA) requirements (products that do will be marked with a stamp). Considering the cost of a visit to the emergency room, it doesn't hurt to purchase an extra pair for the times when a neighbor volunteers to lend a hand or when you misplace the first pair.

The U.S. Occupational Safety and Health Administration (OSHA) recommends that hearing protection be worn when the noise level exceeds 85 decibels (db) for an 8-hour workday. However, considering that a circular saw emits 110 db, even shorter exposure times can contribute to hearing impairment or loss. Both insert and muff-type protectors are available; whichever you choose, be sure that it has a noise reduction rating (NRR) of a least 20 db.

Your construction project will create a lot of sawdust. If you are sensitive to dust, and especially if you are working with pressure-treated wood, it's a good idea to wear a dust mask. Two types of respiratory protection are available: disposable dust masks and cartridge-type respirators. A dust mask is good for keeping dust and fine particles from being inhaled during a single procedure. Respirators have a replaceable filter. Both are available for protection against nontoxic and toxic dusts and mists. Whichever you purchase, be sure that it has been stamped by the National Institute for Occupational Safety and Health/Mine Safety and Health Administration (NIOSH/MSHA) and is approved for your specific operation. When you can taste or smell the contaminate or when the mask starts to interfere with normal breathing, it's time for a replacement.

Work gloves are also nice for avoiding injury to the hands—catching a splinter off a board or developing a blister when digging post holes is not a good way to start a workday. Similarly, heavy-duty work boots will protect your feet. Steel toes will prevent injuries from dropped boards or tools. Flexible steel soles will protect you from puncture by a rogue nail.

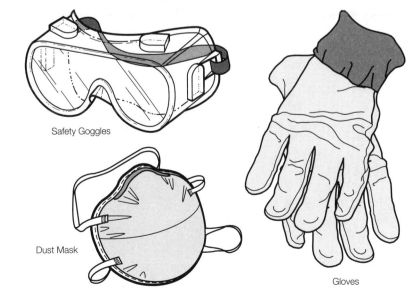

Safety Goggles

Dust Mask

Gloves

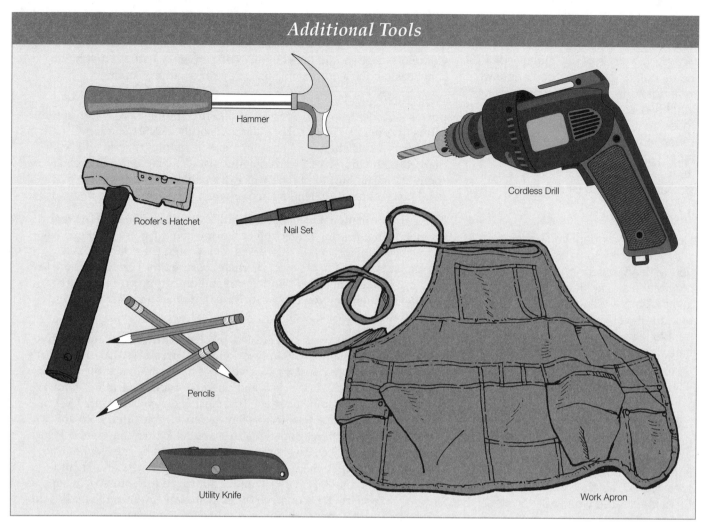

Hammer

Cordless Drill

Roofer's Hatchet

Nail Set

Pencils

Utility Knife

Work Apron

If you're in the market for a second drill, a cordless drill will provide you with all of the attributes of an ordinary drill, but without the hassle of having to drag around a cord. An adjustable clutch is a desirable option, because it will allow you to drive screws to a set depth without overloading the motor or stripping the screwhead.

And how can you build anything without a hammer? You can manage quite well with a standard 16-ounce hammer; a lighter hammer is ideal for fastening railings, trim, and other light members when you are concerned primarily with control. When driving 12d or 16d nails into the beams, or joists, you will quickly learn to appreciate the way a 20-ounce framing hammer can sink a nail in just a few blows. If you are considering roofing your project with wood shingles or shakes, then you will find

that a roofer's hatchet will make that job a lot easier.

One problem with driving nails with a hammer is the "rosettes" that seem to spring up when you are trying to drive the nail flush with the wood. A nail set picks up where most hammers leave off. A nail set is a small shaft of metal with one squre end and the other tapered to a point. The tapered point is sometimes cupped to hold the nailheads. With a nail set, not only can you drive a nail flush with the surrounding wood but you can also countersink nails so that they can be filled with putty to produce a nail-free finish. Nail sets come in various sizes to match different types of nails; use the nail set sized to the nailhead being driven to avoid enlarging the hole.

Unless you want to spend most of the day trying to remember where you left everything, a tool belt or work apron is

a must. A good tool belt will have a spot for your hammer, tape measure, chalkline, and block plane, and still have a pocket left over for nails and screws.

A utility knife will probably be the most reached for tool in either your toolbox or pouch. You will use your utility knife for everything from sharpening your pencil to marking cut lines to cutting shingles to shaving off wood to ease in a close-fitting joint. For general use, you should invest in a fairly heavy-duty knife that has a large angular blade held in place within a hollow metal handle. As with all cutting tools, sharp blades are safest because they provide the most control with the least amount of effort. Discard blades as soon as they're dull.

And there's one thing that a carpenter can never have enough of— pencils, pencils, pencils.

F A S T E N E R S

A gazebo is only as strong as the fasteners that hold it together. Nail, screws, bolts, and specialized framing hardware combine to bind and bond a sturdy project.

Construction Fasteners

Regardless of the type of outdoor structure you're planning to construct, you'll need a variety of nails, bolts, or screws, and some framing hardware to join materials and strengthen joints. Metal fasteners will free you from having to cut and fit complex joints. And considering that cuts made on site are sometimes less than perfect, metal fasteners offer some leeway while still ensuring that the joint will be strong and secure. Some metal fasteners are essential for joining different materials together—no amount of nails can replace a post tie for joining a wooden post onto a concrete footing.

But metal fasteners do have some disadvantages. Large fasteners, such as rafter ties and decking cleats, can save time, but the job will cost you more than if you simply use nails. This price difference can be significant if your project incorporates many metal fasteners into its design. Sometimes metal connectors, even nails, can be visually obtrusive and take away from the overall appearance of a carefully crafted project.

As a general rule, know why and how you are using a fastener for a particular joint, and try to think of possible alternatives.

Nails

The most basic of metal fasteners is the nail. As commonly used, the term penny (abbreviated as d) indicates a nail's length. The number did not originally refer to the length of the nail but to the cost of 100 nails of that size. The length in inches of the various penny sizes of nails are listed in the table on the inside back cover of this book.

The best overall choice for outdoor use is hot-dipped galvanized nails. These nails should be used where rust staining could become a problem. But even though they are coated with a layer of zinc, galvanized nails will rust over time, especially at the exposed nailhead where the coating has been damaged by hammering. You must also be wary of "galvanic corrosion," which can happen any time galvanized nails are used to join a dissimilar metal, particularly in a humid environment. Galvanic corrosion is a reaction between the two metals that creates accelerated weathering at the point of contact. Always select nails that are compatible with any metal being attached to the wood (i.e., use aluminum nails to attach aluminum gutters, copper or brass nails for copper flashing, etc.).

Since they will not rust, stainless-steel and aluminum nails are also suitable for exterior use. Aluminum nails are softer and tend to bend easier than steel nails. Both types of nails are usually more expensive than galvanized nails (stainless-steel nails can be twice as expensive as hot-dipped galvanized), but where excessive corrosion could be a problem, like for a deck near the ocean, it might be the best investment.

Common nails are preferred for general construction because they have an extra-thick shank and a broad head. You can also purchase common nails that have been cement-coated (actually nylon coated) to increase their holding strength. Their coating is melted by the friction of being driven through the wood and quickly resets. Try to drive cement-coated nails home in a few quick blows.

"Deformed" nails, such as screw thread, barbed, or ridged nails, also exhibit greater withdrawal resistance. These nails' shanks have been adapted to increase friction and have a 40 percent greater withdrawal

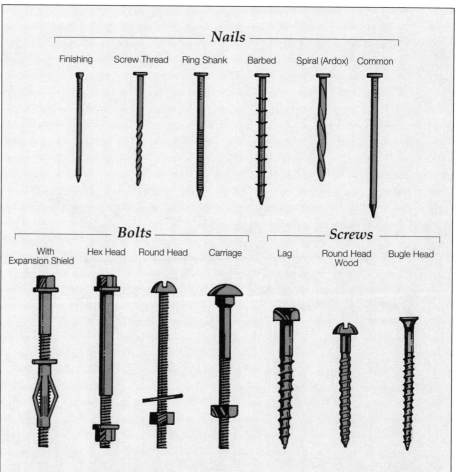

Fasteners. Hundreds of different types and sizes of fasteners are available for securing your project together.

resistance than common nails. These nails are harder to drive.

If you don't want the nail's head to show, choose a finishing nail. Casing nails are similar to finishing nails but have a duller point and thicker shank; they have more holding power than a finishing nail of the same size. After the nail is driven nearly flush, both types can be sunk with a nail set. You can fill the hole with wood putty.

Holding Power

Several characteristics determine the holding power of a nail—its shape, diameter and point (pointed, chisel, or blunt) and the coating of the shank. Think of a nail as a small wedge being driven against the fibers of the wood; anything that would enable this wedge to contact more wood fibers without damaging them or that can attach the wedge more securely to the existing fibers will increase the nail's hold. A thicker nail, for instance, will be more difficult to remove than a thinner nail. The resistance of nails to withdrawal increases almost directly with their diameter; a nail's holding power is doubled with a proportional increase in diameter, because more wood fibers are acting against the wider wedge. Textured or deformed nails have an increased withdrawl resistance compared with smooth-shanked nails. A pointed nail will have a greater resistance because it is driven between wood fibers that a dull nail would tend to sever. And a deformed nail, such as a ring shank or a coated nail will have greater withdrawal resistance than a smooth shank because the wood fibers have a textured surface to grip.

The characteristics of the wood also contribute to overall resistance. Hard, tight-grained woods, such as oak, will grip a nail tighter than a softer wood such as pine. Oak and other hardwoods offer so much resistance that you'll usually have to drill before nailing to drive the nail without bending it. Dry wood will hold a nail better than wet wood. Withdrawal resistance is also determined by how a nail is driven in relation to the wood's

grain—never try to secure anything by nailing into the end of a board.

Using more nails will also increase overall holding strength, just make sure that the nails do not end up splitting the wood. Even slight splitting will greatly affect holding power.

Screws

Bugle-head screws are commonly known as drywall screws because they were originally developed for installing wallboard. These handy screws have become popular for all kinds of woodworking and carpentry projects. Drywall screws have an aggressive thread and do not require a pilot hole. "Bugle Head" refers to the taper beneath the flat head of the screw that allows you to drive them flush in softwood and drywall without drilling a countersink hole.

Screws have greater holding power than nails and can actually pull two boards tightly together. They also create a clean finished appearance by eliminating the possibility of hammer dents and scuffs, and unlike nails, screws will not "pop," or work themselves loose, after a couple of seasons. And since screws can be removed cleanly, they facilitate disassembly or the removal of a damaged board. But, while screws can be used anywhere nails are used in outdoor construction, they cost considerably more than nails. As a result, screws are usually limited to two applications—installing deck boards and finish trim work.

In the United States, drywall screws are most readily available with Phillips heads. Some woodworking supply catalogs offer them with a square recess for driving the screws. Square drive screws are more readily available in Canada. You'll need a power drill or driver to install drywall screws. The square drives are superior because you can't easily strip the drive hole or the bit.

Drywall screws are available in a black oxide finish, suitable for interior

work, and in a hot-dipped galvanized finish, for exterior projects. You'll usually find the exterior version sold as "deck screws." The most common lengths are 1, 1½, 2, 2½, and 3 inches.

If you need to toe-fasten pieces in an area of your project that will be highly visible, you can avoid ugly hammer dents by toe-screwing instead of toe-nailing. Position the boards in place and drill a starter hole with a bit approximately equal in diameter to the shank of the screw.

Sizing Nails and Screws

When determining nail or screw length, the general rule for softwoods is the nail penetration into the bottom piece should be equal to or greater than the thickness of the top piece. For example, if you are nailing 5/4-inch-thick decking boards to joists, 8d nails would do the job. You'll get even better holding power with 10d nails.

When fastening plywood, the choice of the nail depends on the thickness of the panels. For 3/4- and 5/8-inch plywood, use 8d common nails. For 1/2- and 3/8-inch panels use 6d common nails. Space nails every 6 inches along the edges and 12 inches in the field. Ring- or screw-shank nails are recommended for this application to prevent the nails from working their way loose when the wood expands and contracts with moisture changes.

The chart "Nailing Schedule for Light Outdoor Structures" tells you what kind and how many nails to use in the various connections you'll make.

Although not recommended for framing, screws can be used effectively for installing sheathing. For 3/4- to 5/8-inch plywood use a 1½-inch screw. For 1/2- to 3/8-inch plywood use a 1¼-inch screw. Space screws 12 inches along the edges and 24 inches in the field.

Bolts & Rods

The most rigid joint fasteners are bolts and lag screws. These heavy-duty fasteners are recommended for connections that must be extremely strong, such as post-to-beam connections or where a ledger joins to the house. For strength and appearance, a single lag screw or bolt can replace three or four bugle-head screws.

Bolts pass all the way through the pieces they join (or are "through-bolted") and are secured with washers and nuts. The bolt hole diameter should equal the stated diameter of the bolt. Two types of bolts are commonly used in outdoor construction: machine bolts and carriage bolts. Machine bolts resemble lag screws in that they have a hexagonal-shaped head that remains above the surface of the lumber.

Carriage bolts work just like machine bolts, but they have a round head instead of a hex head. Just beneath the head, the shank is square. When tapped into a tight-fitting hole, the square shank seats the bolt into the wood, so that the nut can be tightened. A carriage bolt does not use a washer beneath the head, but a washer is still required beneath the nut. Because the head is pulled almost flush to the surface of the lumber, carriage bolts are typically used on railing posts or in other places where a lag bolt might be visually obtrusive or snag clothing.

Bolt lengths range from 3 to 12 inches, and diameters range from 1/4 tc 3/4 inch in 1/16-inch increments. For longer lengths, you can purchase threaded rod. Bolts should be approximately 1 inch longer than the thickness of the combined pieces to accommodate washers and nuts. Threaded rod uses washers and nuts on both ends, so size it 2 inches longer than the combined thickness. Plan to drill bolt holes using a bit of the same diameter as the bolt. When setting or removing lag or carriage bolts, try not to damage the threads by striking them with a hammer or against a metal surface; damaged threads will make it impossible to thread on the nut. If you must tap the threaded end, protect it with a scrap of wood or hit it with a plastic mallet.

Lag Screws

Lag screws are available in the same size and length as machine or carriage bolts. Because they have a bolt-shaped head, lag screws are

Nailing Schedule for Light Outdoor Structures

Area	Application	Method	Number	Size	Nail Type
Frame	Header to joist	End-nail	3	16d	Common
	Header to sill	Toe-nail	16" oc	10d	Common
	Joist to sill	Toe-nail	2	10d	Common
	Ledger to beam	Face-nail	3/16" oc	16d	Common
	Double top plate	Face-nail	16" oc	10d	Common
	Ceiling joist to top plate	Toe-nail	3	8d	Common
	Rafter to top plate	Toe-nail	2	8d	Common
	Rafter to ceiling joist	Face-nail	5	10d	Common
	Rafter to hip or valley	Toe-nail	3	10d	Common
	Ridge board to rafter	End-nail	3	10d	Common
	Rafter to rafter	Toe-nail	4	8d	Common
	Collar tie (2") to rafter	Face-nail	2	12d	Common
	Collar tie (1") to rafter	Face-nail	3	8d	Common
Roof	Asphalt, new	Face-nail	4	7/8"	Roofing
	Asphalt, reroof	Face-nail	4	1¾"	Roofing
	Wood shingle, new	Face-nail	2	4d	Shingle
	Wood single, reroof	Face-nail	2	6d	Shingle
Sheathing	3/8" plywood	Face-nail	6" oc	6d	Common
	1/2" and thicker plywood	Face-nail	6" oc	8d	Common
	1/2" fiberboard	Face-nail	3" oc	1½"	Roofing
	3/4" fiberboard	Face-nail	3" oc	1¾"	Roofing
	3/4" boards	Face-nail	6" oc	8d	Common

Consult this chart to decide which size and type of nail to use and how many nails to use for the connections you'll make when building your gazebo.

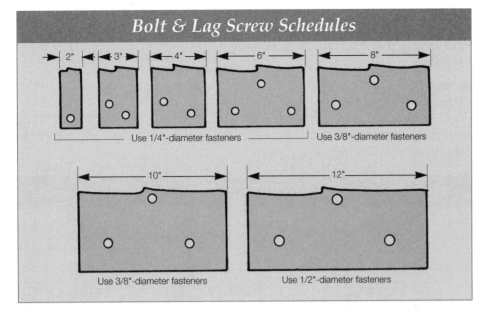

Bolt & Lag Screw Schedules

2"   3"   4"   6"   8"

Use 1/4"-diameter fasteners   Use 3/8"-diameter fasteners

10"   12"

Use 3/8"-diameter fasteners   Use 1/2"-diameter fasteners

sometimes confused with lag bolts, but unlike bolts, they do not protrude through the objects being joined. They're particularly useful in tight spots where you can reach only one side of the connection with a wrench (a socket wrench is easiest). Drill a lead hole about two-thirds the length of the lag screw, using a bit 1/8 inch smaller than the lag screw's shank. Place a washer under each lag screw's head.

It is a better idea to make connections with several small-diameter bolts or lag screws instead of fewer large-diameter bolts. See "Bolt and Lag Screw Schedules" to help you estimate the sizing and spacing for joining boards with lag bolts or screws.

Framing Hardware

You'll find many types of framing connectors in sizes to fit most standard-dimension rough and surfaced lumber. There are several major manufacturers of structural wood fasteners. Their basic product lines cover nearly all applications, but you may need to ask about special fasteners such as the gazebo roof peak fastener, hip rafter ties, or truss plates. Explain your needs to the salesperson. While an effort has been made to select the generic name for the fasteners described in this book,

one manufacturer's hurricane clip may be another's storm tie. The fasteners you do buy may also look a little different from those illustrated. Just make sure they are designed to do the same job.

Remember that most of these fasteners are simply metal accessories designed to assist with, or replace, other traditional joinery techniques. If you cannot find a particular fastener or wish to maintain a metal-free appearance, consider other options.

Nails for Fasteners

Most structural fastener manufacturers also supply nails sized and designed to provide maximum load performance when used with their fasteners. Since they are connecting sheet metal to wood, the nails can be shorter than if you were using a common nail to fasten together two boards of the same thickness. Fastener nails are typically blunted to help eliminate wood splitting. Their surface finish can be galvanized or cement coated to prevent rust.

Use the number of fasteners and nails and the nailing pattern specified by the fastener manufacturer. If specialty nails are not available, use the thickest common nails that will fit through the nailing flange holes. You may have to clinch the nails if they protrude.

Hardware Choices

A. Post Anchors. These connectors secure the base of a load-bearing post to a concrete foundation, slab, or deck. In areas where there is a lot of standing water or rain, choose an elevated post base that raises a post 1 to 3 inches above the surface.

B. Joist Hangers. Joist hangers are used for butt joints between deck joists and beams. Single- and double-size hangers are available. Rafter hangers are similar to joist hangers but are used to hang roof rafters from a ledger board.

C. Saddle Hangers or Purlin Clips. Available in single and double designs, these clips are ideal for installing crosspieces between joists or rafters.

D. Rafter Ties. These ties are used to provide wind and seismic ties for trusses and rafters.

E. Ridge Rafter Connector. These connectors resemble joist hangers with an open bottom. Use them to fasten 2x6 rafters to ridge boards or ledgers. The open bottom can accommodate slopes up to 30 degrees.

F. Truss Plates. These plates are used in the construction of roof trusses. They can be designed with or without a lip. Various sizes are available.

Caution: *Not all plate type fasteners are designed for truss applications. Be sure the plates you buy are specified for roof truss construction. Special truss nails may also be required.*

G. Twist Tie. These straps are ideal for tying pieces that cross at 90 degree angles, such as joists, rafters, and beams.

H. Hip Corner Plate. A hip corner plate connects a rafter or joist to double top plates at a 45 degree angle.

I. Gazebo Roof Peak Tie. Two of these connectors are used at the peak of a six-sided gazebo roof to tie together all rafters. A key block is not needed.

J. Hip Rafter Gazebo Tie. Similar to a hip corner plate, this connector is angled to tie roof rafters to the top plate of a six-sided gazebo.

K. Hurricane Ties. Use these ties to secure rafters and trusses to top plates.

L. Post Caps. These fasteners can be used at the top of a post to join it to a beam or to strengthen a splice connection between two beams.

M. Panel Clips. These clips are slipped between the edges of plywood panels to lock them together where they span between rafters. Panel clips will also help maintain a

sufficient gap between panels to allow for thermal expansion.

N. Stair Angles. These clips support treads, eliminating the need for notching stringers.

Framing Hardware

TECHNIQUES

Using proper construction techniques is essential for safety as much as for structural stability. There is a right way and a wrong way to attach boards, cut lumber, and create joints. This chapter will show you the proper methods.

Proper Building Techniques

Every carpenter has his or her own approach to a job. However, if you were to watch several people, you would start to notice similarities in the ways they get the job done. Many of these similarities evolve through trial and error. By working on your own, you too will eventually learn that certain systems work better than others.

But you don't need to learn everything from the school of hard knocks. Starting off with a few basic techniques will provide you with a solid foundation to successfully (and enjoyably) build your project right on the first try, with a minimum of wasted time and materials. Some of these suggestions may seem to be common sense—the point is to learn to think like a carpenter. In time, you will come to use some of these suggestions reflexively.

Planning a Work Space

The phrase "a place for everything and everything in its place" is not reserved solely for the Shakers. Good carpenters appreciate and abide by this well-worn saying.

Think back to your last project. Chances are you probably wasted far too much time looking for a screwdriver, trying to find a free receptacle to plug another tool in, or carrying wood from one side of the yard to the other. And then there were the half dozen trips to the hardware store. When you work this way, even the smallest project will devour the entire weekend. Planning out your project in relation to your tools and work space is an excellent way of making more efficient use of your time.

A well-planned work site is a lot safer too. For example, placing a few sawhorses or a chop saw right next to the stack of lumber will take the strain off of your back by minimizing the times you have to drag those 16-foot boards across the length of the site. Centralizing power tools in one corner also centralizes power cords, which could save you from tripping over the one that you "don't know how it got there in the first place."

Sometimes a quick sketch is all that it takes to visualize how everything will be able to work best on a given job. Plan how you want your site to work. Include all the major elements

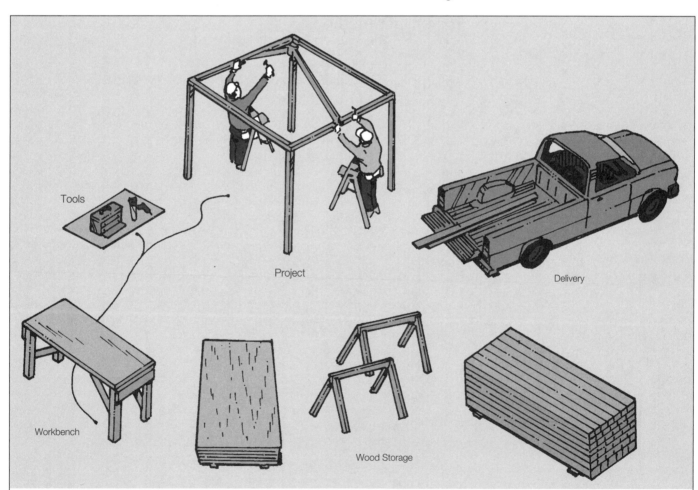

Tools

Project

Delivery

Workbench

Wood Storage

Planning a Work Space. In an efficient work site tools and materials are strategically placed to conserve steps while allowing you room to work.

of construction: where you can park your car or truck, where the wood will be delivered, where the electrical cords are running from, and of course, the location of your project's foundation. Try to imagine how these elements will work with each other, and plan the work space accordingly. For example, if you are handling delivery of wood on your own, you will naturally want to keep wood-toting to a minimum. Make preliminary cuts near the side of the stack before carrying the boards to the foundation. Make sure that you'll be able to supply enough electricity at the cutting site. If you are working in an area that's inaccessible to extension cords, you might have to rent a generator for a few days. Planning out the site this way is an excellent way of identifying and solving problems before you begin.

Besides your time, your greatest investment in this project is wood. Be sure to stack your pile neatly to avoid unnecessary damage to the material as well as to your workers. The weight from a properly stacked pile will prevent boards from cupping and warping. Centralizing all the material in one corner will prevent a lot of accidents throughout construction. Cutoffs and sawdust will also be centralized in one corner, which should make cleanup a little easier. Restacking your material gives you an opportunity to select pieces for special applications, such as railings and trim.

Nailing & Drilling

There's a little more to nailing than just a well-aimed blow.

The structural strength of your project depends on using the right size and number of nails in the right locations.

Splitting

Splitting is not a major problem with softwoods. But woods without a uniform texture, such as southern yellow pine and Douglas fir do split more than the uniformly textured woods such as northern and Idaho white pine, sugar pine and ponderosa pine. And all boards have a tendency to split near the end. Even a minor split will affect the holding power of the nail and the overall strength of the joint.

Skewing. Skewed nails are driven in at opposing angles to hook the boards together.

If you use several nails at a single joint, stagger their positions. Another way to avoid splitting is to drill holes 75 percent of the nail diameter or to switch to a smaller diameter nail. You can also reduce the chance of splitting by blunting the tip of the nail. Remember that a blunt point destroys wood fibers and will result in a reduced withdrawal resistance.

Skewing

Skewing creates a sounder connection by "hooking" the boards together as well as by reducing the possibility of splitting. You can do this by simply driving the nails in at opposing angles.

Clinching

If nails go completely through both boards, you have three possible options. You could simply use shorter nails, or you could try driving the longer nail at an angle, to make it travel through more wood. A third alternative is to "clinch" the nails, or to bend over the exposed tip. Although it's not the most attractive option, clinching increases holding strength as much as 170 percent over unclinched nails.

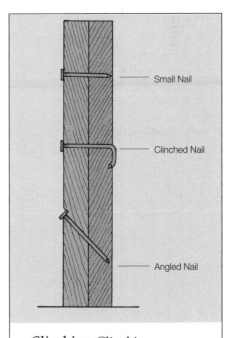

Small Nail

Clinched Nail

Angled Nail

Clinching. Clinching ensures that a nail cannot work itself loose.

Toe-Nailing

Most of the time, when two boards need to be joined at a right angle, you can nail through the face of one board into the end of the other. But sometimes, the face you would prefer to nail into is inaccessible or the piece you have to nail through is too thick. For example, you can't nail through a 4x4 post to attach a hand-rail. In cases like this, you need to toe-nail the pieces together. Toe-nailing means joining two boards by nailing at an angle through the end, or toe, of one board into the face of another. Position the nail on the first piece at least 1½ inches from the second piece. Start the nail at a 60- to 75-degree angle. When it is started, adjust it to a 30- to 40-degree angle. Move your hand and drive the nail home. If it is possible, drive another nail on the other side of the board as well to increase hold-ing power.

Screwing

Considering the popularity of cordless drills and drivers on today's construction sites, you probably will

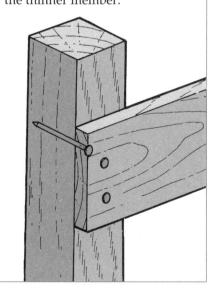

be using a few screws in addition to nails to put your project together. Screwing boards together does have its advantages. First, screws have a way of "pulling" two boards together to make a tighter-fitting joint. Using a driver also enables you to drive screws accurately in spots where you don't have the room to swing a ham-mer. Also, because of their threads, screws grip better than nails. At the same time, screws are easier to re-move—just flip your driver in reverse.

It does take a little practice before you can drive a Phillips head screw at high speeds without stripping the screw head or the driver bit (buy a couple of #2 Phillips head bits just in case). When driving screws with a driver, start at a slow speed until the screw takes hold and increase the speed until the screw is set. Main-tain constant pressure parallel to the screw and avoid stopping before it is in all the way. Friction exerted on these fasteners can sometimes catch the screw, and you may snap it if you allow the wood fibers time to bind. When the head has countersunk itself into the wood, lift the driver as you take your finger off the trigger. If your driver has an automatic clutch, you don't have to worry as much about stripping or snapping the screw, the clutch will disengage the driver when the screw is at the correct depth.

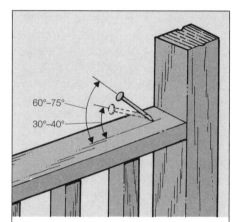

Toe-Nailing. Decrease the driving angle after you start the toe-nail.

Screwing. Maintain pressure through the screw to drive it straight and prevent slippage.

Cutting with a Circular Saw

You'll probably pick up the circular saw almost as frequently as your hammer. The tool is capable of performing very straight, precise cuts suitable for all types of joinery as well as decorative ornamentation. The most elaborate effects are simply variations of a few basic cuts.

Choosing the Blade

It goes without saying that carbide-tipped blades are far better than steel blades. Although they cost a bit more, carbide stays sharp five times longer than steel—a definite advantage when cutting dense (and usually wet) wood like pressure-treated southern pine. A sharp blade also puts less stress on your saw's motor and reduces the chance of binding or kickback.

But which type of carbide-tipped blade should you buy? For these projects, you should be able to do all of your cutting with an 18- to 24-tooth combination blade. "Combination" means that it cuts well perpendicular and parallel to the grain. This blade also works fine when cutting posts and plywood. A coarser blade is designed for rough work, like demolition, and will produce a splintery cut. A blade with 36 or more teeth is too fine for this kind of construction and may tend to bind in wet wood.

Although a top-of-the-line blade may cut cleaner and stay sharper than a less expensive blade, and unless you are willing to have the blade professionally resharpened, you might be better off with a middle-of-the-line model. A new less expensive carbide blade will out perform even the best blade after it has chewed through a whole stack of wet wood or snagged a nail. Some very good 24-tooth blades can be purchased for less than half of the price of the premiums. And why pay for a sharpener (if you can find one) when it's cheaper and easier just to buy a new blade?

Kickback is the term describing that dreaded action when the saw suddenly kicks backward in the middle of a cut. What happens is that the teeth on the rear part of the blade catch the edge of the saw cut, causing the saw to jump out of the kerf. The threat is that the saw could buck up or perhaps even run backward toward you before you could release the switch. As soon as you feel the saw start to kick back, stop and correct the problem before continuing.

Leading Causes of Kickback:

- **Binding Board.** Sometimes the stresses in the wood cause the kerf to close. Binding also will occur if the cutoff is not falling free and is pinching the blade.

- **Twisting Blade.** A circular saw is not a jigsaw. If for whatever reason you started your cut off the line, do not try to correct your error in midcut. Stop the saw and start the cut over.

- **Backing Up the Blade.** Don't do it. Always stop the blade before backing up the saw.

- **Dull Blade.** A dull blade will heat up and bind, which could cause it to kick back. It pays to have a spare blade handy.

Unfortunately, kickback is the nature of the beast, and it happens even to experienced carpenters. For this reason, it's important always to keep your hands well away from the blade or cut path and position yourself to one side of the cut—never directly behind it.

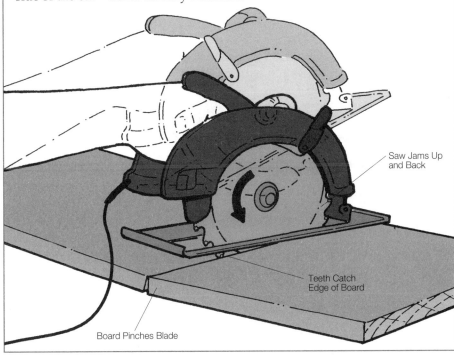

Saw Jams Up and Back

Teeth Catch Edge of Board

Board Pinches Blade

Your saw will tell you when it's time to switch blades. Some indications of a dull blade include a slower cut speed, a "strained" motor sound, splintery cuts, and even smoking or burned cuts.

Squaring the Blade

No matter what circular saw you have, you can't expect the angle markings stamped on the saw to be accurate. To ensure square cuts, use a square to set the blade.

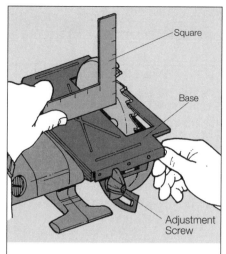

1 Use an angle square or a try square to ensure that the blade of the saw is square to the base.

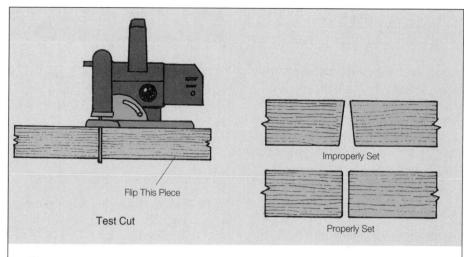

Test Cut

Flip This Piece

Improperly Set

Properly Set

2 Two test cuts on a piece of scrap will let you know if your saw blade is perfectly square to the saw base.

1 Squaring the Blade to the Base. Unplug the saw. Now turn the saw over and loosen the angle adjustment. Set an angle square or try square against the blade and the base. Make sure you hold the square against the body of the blade without touching the teeth. The teeth are offset from the body and will throw off your adjustment. Tighten the angle adjustment when the blade and base bear evenly on the square.

2 Testing for Squareness. Crosscut a small block off a scrap piece of 2x4. Flip the block and match the piece, cut edge to cut edge, with the 2x4. If your blade is not square to the base, you'll see a gap equal to twice the amount your blade is out of square. If you see a gap, repeat Step 1 and try again. When the cut edges meet squarely, the blade is square to

the base. Check the stamped markings on your saw. You might want to make your own square mark with a scribe or small file.

Making Square & Accurate Cuts

1 Positioning the Workpiece. Before making the cut, your workpiece must be well supported on a stable surface that won't move during the cut. To avoid dangerous kickback, you must ensure that the piece you are cutting off can fall away without binding. If you are trimming a small piece off a board, position the board across two sawhorses and make the cut to the outside of one of the horses, never between the horses.

When the piece being cut off is too long to let fall on the ground, you

can do your cutting right on top of a stack of wood, as long as the stack is neat and stable.

2 Aligning the Blade to the Line. Use a square to strike a line where you want to cut the board. Make sure the workpiece is well supported on a stable surface and that the waste piece will be able to fall away without binding the blade at the end of the cut.

As mentioned, the teeth on a circular saw blade are offset. One tooth is offset to the left, the next to the right and so on in an alternating pattern. Position the saw blade along the waste side of your cut line. Select a tooth that's offset toward the cut line and align the saw so that tooth just touches the line.

1 Whether you do your cutting on a saw horse (left) or right on top of the lumber stack (right), make sure the work surface is stable.

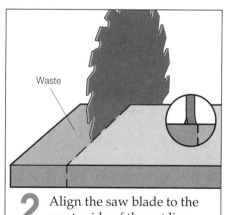

Waste

2 Align the saw blade to the waste side of the cut line.

3 An angle square is helpful for making crosscuts.

Using a Rip Guide. Use a rip guide to make rip cuts with the circular saw.

3 **Making the Cut.** With just a little bit of practice you'll be able to cut squarely by following a pencil line. Get in the habit of keeping your eye on the leading edge of the blade, not the little notch or mark on the front of the saw base.

If you are new to using a circular saw, you might want to use your angle square as a guide until you get a feel for the saw. Even when you gain confidence, this is a useful technique for joinery cuts that will show in the final project; for example the end cut on a rail that will meet a post. You can also use the angle square to make accurate 45 degree miter cuts with the circular saw.

First, use the square to mark the cut line. Slide the square back onto the piece you mean to use and hold it firmly with one hand against the edge of the stock. Set the base of your saw so that its edge bears against the square edge of the angle square. Adjust the saw and the square's position until the saw blade lines up with the cut line. Brace the square against the stock and make the cut, using the square's edge as a guide. Saw with a light, steady pressure, allowing the blade to set the feed rate.

Using a Rip Guide. When ripping lumber, you should use a rip guide. This is a steel guide that attaches to the base with a thumbscrew. The guide has a shoe that runs along the side of the board as you cut it along its length.

Cutting Plywood. Cutting plywood is the exception to the free-fall rule. Un-less it is properly supported, the cut-off always binds as it falls away. The easiest way to avoid this is to cut large sheets of plywood right on the floor. Support the sheet with 2x4s. This way, you can stand on the plywood and "walk-through" the cut. It is also a lot safer; a long cutoff section can't fall, splinter, bind, or cause kickback.

Setting the Depth of the Cut

To use a circular saw safely and produce the cleanest possible cut, you want to set the blade so that it just penetrates the other side and clears itself of wood chips with the least amount of blade. The deeper the blade is set, the more heat it generates and the greater the risk of binding and kicking back, especially when cutting tricky materials like plywood. Set the saw blade depth about 1/4 inch deeper than the thickness of the wood.

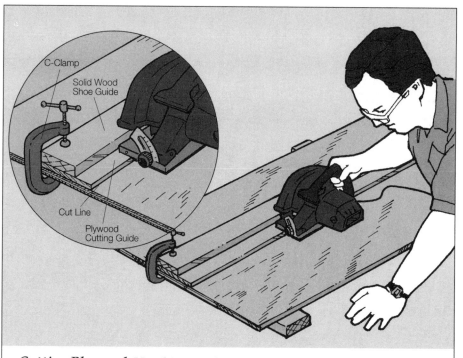

Cutting Plywood. Use this straight cutting jig when ripping plywood.

One way to guide a saw through an accurate rip is to use a straight cutting jig. Simply tack a thin strip of hardboard or plywood to the bottom of a straight length of 1-by stock. Using the 1-by as a guide, cut off the excess plywood to determine the exact cut line. Clamp or tack nail the jig directly to the sheet you are cutting.

Circular Saw Joinery

One way to gauge the level of craftsmanship used in a project is to inspect the ways the builder joined one board to another. Skillful joinery has been used for many hundreds of years to join wood members—long before the invention of nails and screws. Besides being visually attractive, these techniques produce joints that are stronger than simply nailing one board to another. These joints

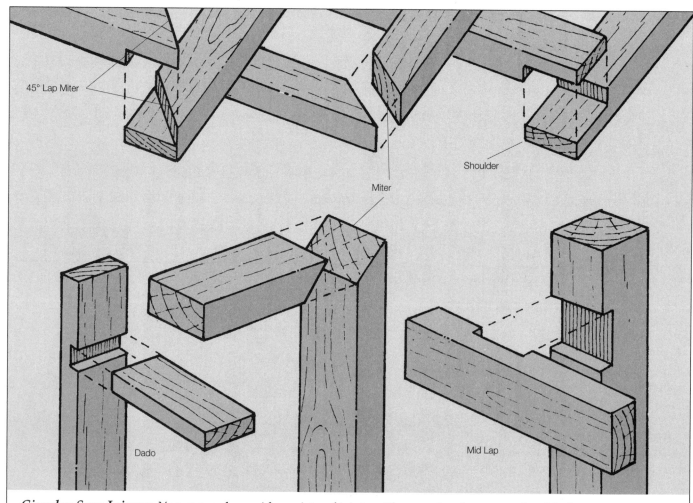

Circular Saw Joinery. You can make a wide variety of joints with your circular saw and a chisel.

will take some time to produce, but by working with a circular saw, you should have no problems cutting them quickly and consistently.

Miter joints can be cut in one pass. Notches, lap joints, and dadoes require three separate steps: kerfing, roughing out, and paring.

1 **Kerfing the Joint.** Lay out the shoulders of the notch, lap joint, or dado you wish to cut. Adjust the saw to the depth you want the joint to be. (It's a good idea to make a test cut to make sure your setting is right.)

Make a series of closely spaced kerfs in the waste area of the joint. The first and last kerfs should be made with a angle square to ensure that the shoulder is square, all the other kerfs need not be precise since you are just cutting wood out of the notch.

2 **Roughing Out the Joint.** Rough out the joint by chiseling out the waste. At this point, hit the chisel with a hammer to break the pieces free, but keep the chisel bevel pointing down to control the depth of cut. Chisel to the bottom of the joint in the center, leaving the edges high.

3 **Paring Out the Joint.** With the chisel's bevel pointing up, pare away leftover ridges. Work from the outside edges in to the center. Use one hand to push the chisel into the waste and use the other to keep the back of the chisel flat against the wood.

1 Set the circular saw to the depth of the notch, then make several kerfs between the shoulders.

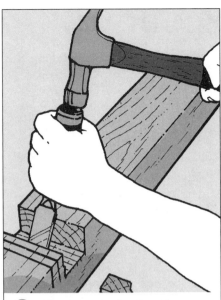

2 Chop out the kerfs with a hammer and chisel.

3 Pare away leftover ridges with the chisel.

Fighting Crooked Stock

The challenge of carpentry is that you are trying to make something straight and square out of a natural material that resists our best efforts to make it regular. Almost every board you use will be at least slightly crooked, cupped, or twisted. Carpentry is a constant battle to wedge and nail pieces of wood into the position and shape you want them to take. A smart carpenter uses the forces within the board to his or her advantage.

Crowning. The most common example is "crowning" horizontal structural members such as beams and joists. This means to sight along the edges of a board to decide which way it bows. Then

Crowning. Look down one edge of the board to see if it is straight, bowed, or crooked.

When you use lumber decking boards, you need to leave a small space between each board for appearance and to let water through. One way to gauge the space is with the body of a 10d or 16d common nail. The problem with this method is you wind up spending a lot of time fetching nails that fell through the spaces. Here is a handy spacer jig that will eliminate that problem.

All you have to do is rip a strip of wood at the desired gap thickness (about 1/8 inch). Tack the strip to a wider piece of scrap as shown.

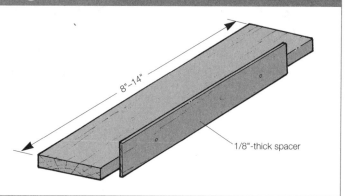

8"–14"

1/8"-thick spacer

install the board with the convex edge facing up. This gives the board a head start in resisting sagging from the weight bearing on it.

If you are installing decking boards, there is no way to use crook to your advantage. If a board is badly crooked, use it to make short pieces.

But if the crook is mild, there are a few ways to force it into place.

Maximize your straightening leverage by first fastening the straightest end of the board to at least two joists. Position the board so that the curve bends out—away from the decking boards that have already been installed.

One method is to use a pipe clamp to pull the board straight. Concentrate on straightening the board on a joist-by-joist basis. As soon as the board is properly positioned, nail it into place and reposition the clamp as necessary to gain more leverage.

Another way of doing the same thing is to screw a temporary plank onto the joists in front of the crooked board. The brace should be positioned at an angle that approximates that of the wedge. Use a wooden wedge to force the plank into position. It is also possible to lever the board straight with a length of 2x4. Never use a pry bar to force a board into position. The metal can dig into the wood or dent the edge of the decking.

How to Straighten Crooked Stock

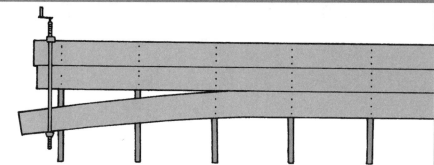

Pull boards straight with a pipe clamp if it is close to the edge of the deck.

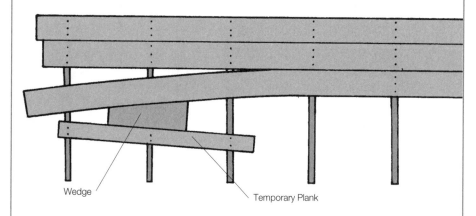

Wedge

Temporary Plank

Wedge crooked boards in place with a temporary plank and a tapered piece of scrap.

Putting the Good Side Up

Some carpenters believe that deck boards will shed water better if installed with the bark side down because boards will cup to shed water that way. Others prefer bark side up because boards installed bark side down will suffer more from grain raising and splitting along the annular rings.

The U.S. Department of Agriculture's Forest Products Laboratory has tested both these theories. Their conclusion is, it doesn't matter which way the boards are laid. The laboratory's recommendation is simply to place the most attractive side of the board up.

G R O U N D W O R K

Every structure needs a firm footing. So that you can provide this footing, the basics of masonry work is explained in this chapter. You'll lay site lines, prepare a foundation site, pour concrete footings, and build a strong base for your gazebo.

Preparing the Site

Begin your project with foundation work that is accurate and strong, and the rest of the construction process will be a pleasure. For the projects in this book, accurate foundation work means getting support posts firmly set in exactly the right positions. If you get the post support positions wrong, you'll spend the rest of the project compensating for it. Strong foundation work means the posts must be firmly anchored either in the ground or in concrete. If you decide instead to rest your project on a slab, the post anchor bolts must be accurately placed and the concrete surfaced to a smooth, hard finish.

Clear the construction area. Remove all shrubs, rocks, and other obstacles that are not part of your design. Rake up all loose twigs and leaves.

It is not always necessary to strip away low grass and ground cover before building wood deck projects, such as a gazebo. Any grass covered by the deck will die from lack of sun. However, a little landscaping now will ensure a better looking site that will be easier to maintain later. Once the footings are in place, lay down a layer of landscaping fabric right on top of the grass and cover it with 2 to 4 inches of gravel or wood chips. Landscaping fabric is preferable to covering the ground with 6-mil polyethylene. Both materials will keep weeds from sprouting and will provide a clean, finished appearance, but the fabric will also allow water to percolate through to the soil, preventing puddling or washout.

If you plan to set your project on a concrete slab, you will have to strip away grass and other ground cover and excavate to the necessary depth. Concrete must be placed on firm, compacted soil.

Slope & Drainage

You don't need to worry about slope when building a project that has a wood deck. That's because water drains through the cracks between

Preparing the Site. Cover the ground under your project with landscaping fabric and wood chips to discourage weeds and prevent washout (left). Remove sod and soil and level out the excavation before pouring a concrete slab (right).

deck boards or is shed by the roof. A concrete slab, however, should slope slightly, or have a slight crown, to ensure proper drainage. Slope is important for gazebo projects to prevent water from puddling and eventually causing water damage to the concrete itself. A slope of 1/8 to 1/4 inch per foot is sufficient. To determine just how the pitch will affect the overall layout of your slab, multiply the length of the run in feet by 0.25. That number indicates in inches how much your slab must vary from level over the course of the entire run.

Some carpenter's levels have two sets of lines on each vial. The second set of lines is used by plumbers to ensure proper drainage when running pipes; when the bubble touches the outside line, the slope is at 1/4 inch per foot. You can also use this tool to determine the correct pitch for

Checking Slope

One way to determine slope is to first string a level line with the top of the form. At the far side of the board or form measure down from the string to the desired slope. (For example, you would have to measure down 2½ inches from level to give a 10-foot span a slope of 1/4 inch per foot.) Mark the desired slope with another string.

your project. First string a level line starting from the highest point of the form. Next, use the level to determine the slope. Hold one end of the level against the high side of the form next to the string and lower the other end until the bubble touches the outside line. Mark this slope with another string. This method is not as accurate

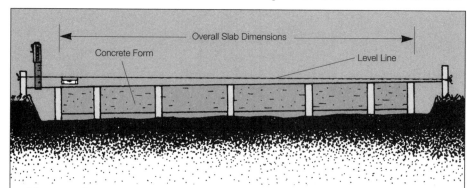

Slope and Drainage. Concrete slabs are designed with a slight slope of 1/8 to 1/4 in. per foot to avoid puddling.

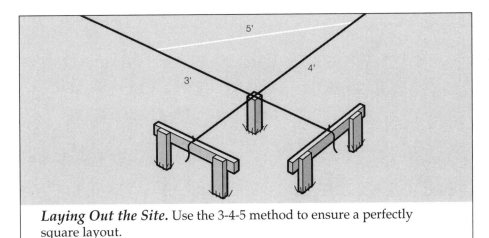

Laying Out the Site. Use the 3-4-5 method to ensure a perfectly square layout.

as measuring the slope off of a level line, but it is a quick way of double-checking your calculations.

If any roof gutters empty into or near the project area, try to angle the downspouts to direct the runoff away from the deck. If that is not practical, you might have to install an underground line to drain water away from the area.

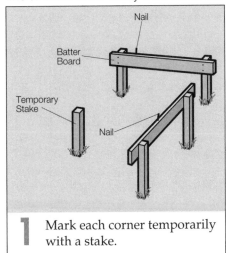

1 Mark each corner temporarily with a stake.

Laying Out the Site

All of the gazebos in this book, including the six- and eight-sided gazebos, begin with either a square or rectangular layout. You can easily check a project for square using the 3-4-5 layout method. Simply remember that if one side of a right triangle measures 3 feet and another measures 4 feet, the hypotenuse must measure 5 feet. If any of these measurements are off, the corner is not a true right angle. The same rule holds true for multiples of these dimensions. A right triangle with sides measuring 6 and 8 feet will have a hypotenuse of 10 feet.

1 **Roughing Out the Dimensions.** Use a tape measure to rough out the perimeter dimensions of the project. Drive in temporary stakes at each corner.

Erect batter boards at right angles to each other about 2 feet outside the rough corner locations of the slab foundation or deck. These batter boards provide support for guide strings and a location to mark out key dimensions. The batter boards can be any scrap stock as long as they are about 2 feet long. Support each batter board with two short stakes. Use a line level to set the batter board crosspieces at the same height.

2 **Stringing the Lines.** Set up guide lines to outline the entire slab or deck. Check that the line is level and secure it to the batter boards.

Make right angles at each corner by using the 3-4-5 triangle method. Measure from point A on the first stake along the line 3 feet and mark point B. Run a second line perpendicular to the first across point A. Mark point C 4 feet from point A. Move line AC so that the distance BC is exactly 5 feet. Angle BAC is now a 90-degree angle.

With all four string lines in place, double-check squareness by measuring the diagonals between opposing corners. The measurements should be equal. If they are not, recheck your layout.

3 **Reposition Corner Stakes.** Accurately reposition the temporary corner stakes using a plumb bob to transfer the point of intersection to the ground.

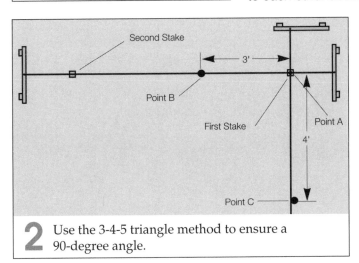

2 Use the 3-4-5 triangle method to ensure a 90-degree angle.

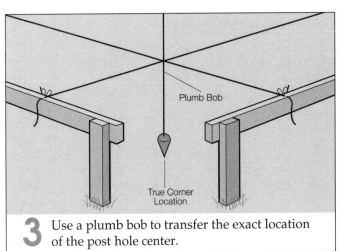

3 Use a plumb bob to transfer the exact location of the post hole center.

Setting Posts

Projects that do not use a slab foundation require the setting of posts firmly in the ground or on concrete footings. You can use a clamshell-type posthole digger to dig holes for the footings or posts. If many holes are needed, renting a gasoline-powered auger-type digger will certainly speed up the work. You can rent either one- or two-man models; the size you choose depends on the number of holes that you have to dig and the soil conditions of the area. The manager of your rental store will be able to suggest which one will best meet your specific needs. Be sure to read and follow safety directions for all power machinery, and be aware of any hidden utility lines, such as gas and water.

To prevent frost heave, your footing should extend below the frost line. Follow local building codes concerning the depth and diameter of the footing or post placement.

Placing Posts Directly in the Ground

As a general rule, when setting posts directly in the ground, the post hole should be about three times the width of the post. It should also extend into the ground at least one-third the overall post height. For example, if you need 8 feet of post above ground level, you should buy a 12-foot post and dig the holes 4 feet deep. These are only general guidelines; always check with your building inspector before deciding how deep to sink your posts.

Compact the base of the hole and add 6 inches of gravel to help drainage. Place the post in the hole. For posts set in the ground, you should always use pressure-treated wood.

Premixed bag concrete is the most convenient method of setting posts in the ground. Fast-setting mixes are available that set up in minutes and reach final set in several hours. With some brands, installation can be as

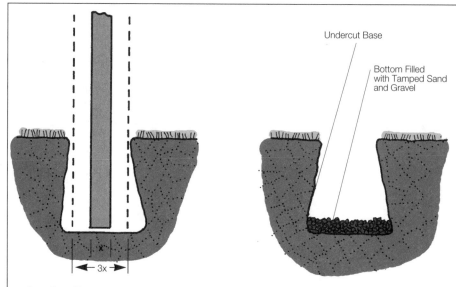

Undercut Base

Bottom Filled with Tamped Sand and Gravel

Setting Posts. Set posts according to the "Rule of Three." The hole should be three times the width and one-third the length of the post.

simple as positioning the post and adding layers of dry mix and water until the hole is filled. Follow the concrete manufacturer's directions.

Slope the top of the concrete away from the post to drain water. Use a level to check for plumb and brace the post firmly with lengths of scrap lumber and recheck.

Post Footings

Another method of securing posts is to use metal post anchors set in concrete footings. Metal post anchors require the same amount of preparation as sinking posts in concrete. Both require footings dug below the frost line. However, since only the metal fastener is sunk into the concrete, you can use shorter post lengths to reach a given height, making it the most economical choice for building a gazebo.

A post anchor does not offer the same amount of lateral strength as sinking a post, so you wouldn't want to use anchors for a fence. But posts tied into a gazebo or other structure with four or more sides don't have to handle a significant lateral load.

The hole diameter for a 4x4 post should be approximately 12 inches. In firm soil, concrete can be placed directly in the hole. Place a 6-inch layer of gravel in the base of the hole and fill it with concrete. When mixed to the proper consistency, the concrete will find its own level. Insert the post anchor before the concrete sets up. Work quickly if you are using fast-setting concrete. Use a torpedo level to make sure that the connector is plumb. This is a critical point in the project, so check your work several times and be sure anchors do not shift or sag.

Remember Post Dimensions

Keep in mind that for some projects the distance between foundation post locations does not equal the overall length or width of the project. But it's easier and more accurate to lay out the perimeter post locations and allow for slight overhang than it is to lay out the true perimeter and adjust inward. For all projects, check your plans carefully and measure along guide lines to determine all key dimensions.

In loose soil, you may have to dig a slightly larger hole and set a wood form over it so that 5 or 6 inches of concrete are located above ground.

Ready-Made Forms. Another alternative is to use a ready-made form available at most building supply stores. Simply cut the cylindrical cardboard form to length with a handsaw or saber saw and insert it into the hole. You can use the form to make the footing flush to the ground. Or, if you are placing posts in a wet area, you can leave the forms longer to create concrete piers a few inches above ground level. Any cardboard that protrudes from the ground can be trimmed away after the concrete hardens.

If you are building a small structure in a region with little or no frost-heaving problem, you may not need a footing. Check with your building inspector. It may be permissible to place your project on precast concrete pier blocks. Pier blocks are available with post connectors already set in place. They create a wider, firmer base than a post set directly on the ground, and prevent moisture problems by keeping the post out of the dirt.

Most water damage can be avoided simply by raising the posts off their anchors by less than 1/4 inch. Cut a double-thick scrap of asphalt shingle to serve as a spacer.

Concrete Slabs

A concrete deck, or slab, is a great base for a gazebo. A 4-inch-thick slab set 1½ to 2 inches above ground level is suitable for most outdoor projects. To provide drainage under the concrete, a 4- to 6-inch-thick subbase of 1-inch crushed stone is recommended in all but the driest of climates. Add 2 inches of sand or rock dust over the gravel to improve drainage and help level the

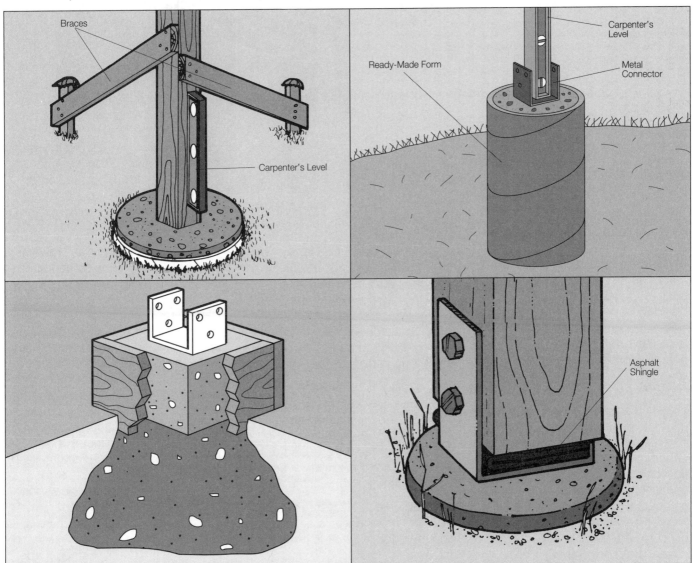

Post Footings. Keep posts plumb with temporary braces (top left). Install the metal anchor as soon as the concrete will support its weight (top right). Use wood forms to retain concrete shape (bottom left). Place an asphalt shingle under the post for protection against water damage (bottom right).

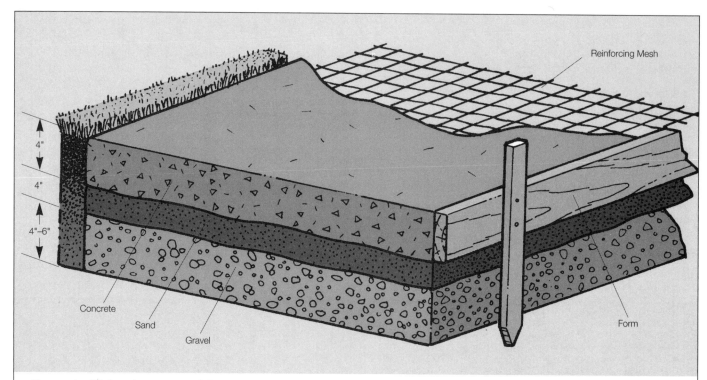

Concrete Slabs. A concrete slab is only as good as its foundation. Sand and gravel subbases help improve drainage and ensure a level pour.

Labels in figure: 4", 4", 4"–6", Reinforcing Mesh, Concrete, Sand, Gravel, Form

subbase to ensure an even layer of concrete. Wire mesh reinforcement is recommended in climates subject to freeze-thaw cycles.

For outdoor slabs, plastic sheathing is not needed over the subgrade or subbase. The plastic would prevent excess water from leaving the fresh slab, bringing it to the surface as bleed water. On the surface, the bleed water will get in the way of finishing operations. It's better just to cast the slab on earth or on a porous subbase.

Estimating Amounts

The standard unit of measure in the concrete industry is the cubic yard. To estimate the amount of concrete needed, just multiply the thickness (in inches) of the slab by its width and length in feet and divide this number by 12. This gives you cubic feet. Divide the number of cubic feet by 27 to find the number of cubic yards. The chart "Cubic Yards of Concrete Used in Slab Construction" on page 33, lists amounts needed for common slab areas.

Form Work

The wood form work for slabs must be strong and stable. Use simple butt joints at all corners, and stake and nail the forms firmly in place. Most form work for slabs is constructed of 2-by framing lumber set on edge. Because a 2x4 is only 3½ inches wide, rake the sand or rock dust subbase along the perimeter to raise it 1/2 inch off the subgrade and create a true 4-inch-deep form. Backfill the gap at the bottom of the form to prevent leakage.

After placing the gravel and sand or rock dust in place, lay down the wire mesh. Set the mesh on small stones or bits of brick and locate it in the center of the slab. Overlay individual pieces and keep the mesh at least 6 inches from the edge of the slab.

In areas subject to severe temperatures and frost heave, large slabs need an edge stiffener to prevent chipping and breaking. The easiest way to do this is to build permanent wood forms instead of temporary ones. Use pressure-treated wood for this, so the frame won't rot away.

Strips can also be installed in the body of the slab to serve as control joints. Mask the tops of the boards with tape during the pour to protect them from stains and abrasion from the concrete.

When pouring a large slab, you may choose to install some screed guides to help you level off the concrete. As with edge guides, you can choose to install temporary guides that can be removed as soon as that section has been screeded or permanent guides that can also serve as control joints for the slab. Screed guides are 2x4s supported on stakes. Permanent guides must be level with the tops of the forms and should be spaced evenly every 8 to 10 feet. For temporary screed guides, place one end of the 2x4 guide on top of the form, level it, and stake it into place. Work from the other side and repeat this process so that the guides meet in the center. With the screed guides in place, you will need a screed made from 2x4s. For the temporary guides, nail a 1x2 block to the top end of the screed, which will ride on the temporary guide. The other end of the screed

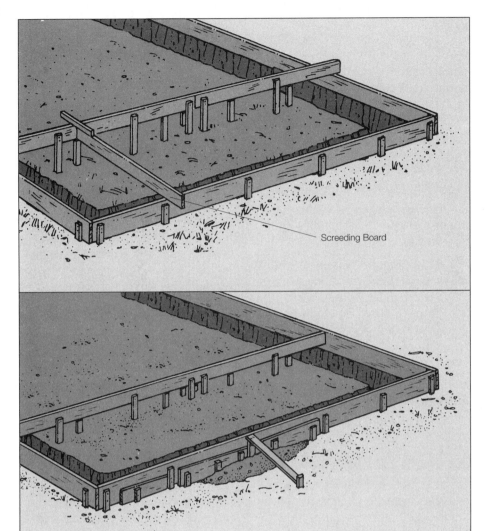

Screeding Board

Form Work. Remove temporary forms as soon as possible. Fill stake holes with concrete (top). Permanent forms serve as control joints for the finished slab (bottom).

entails. You won't be able to handle a large volume of truck-delivered ready-mix concrete working alone. Assemble a crew of at least two helpers. Always have at least one helper with some experience in floating, final troweling, and edging. An experienced concrete finisher will keep the project moving and serve as an adviser to less experienced crew members. Another idea is for you to do all the preparation—layout, form building, and subgrade preparation—and then hire a professional to handle the actual concrete work.

If you plan to do the work yourself, discuss the project with someone at the ready-mix plant. He or she should know the local codes and the concrete specifications used in your area. Also be sure to check with the building inspector. You'll probably need a permit, and the inspector can let you know in advance if your plans follow code. Plan ahead for choice delivery times, such as Saturday mornings, and know the procedure for canceling delivery if the weather fails to cooperate. Be sure the truck will have access to your site. A delivery truck can tear up a lawn or sink into fresh fill.

Plan to work in good weather—late spring and early fall are ideal times for large concrete projects. At these times of the year there's usually no threat of freezing or drying out the concrete. Also, your workers won't have to contend with the hot summer sun.

rides on top of the form. For center screeds, use blocks on both ends of the screed. Remove the screed guides and fill in the stake holes after the concrete has been poured.

If you are pouring a slab against the house for an attached project, remember to pitch the slab away from the house at a slope of 1/8 inch per running foot. Check for proper pitch after the forms and gravel base are in place. An expansion joint is needed where the slab abuts the structure. Control joints should be spaced 8 to 10 feet.

Delivery Considerations

One of the quickest and most economical ways to obtain several

yards of uniformly mixed concrete is to work with a concrete supplier. But you should take a little time to consider exactly what this step of the job

Cubic Yards of Concrete Used in Slab Construction

Square Feet	Thickness of Slab (Inches)		
	4	5	6
25	0.31	0.39	0.46
50	0.62	0.77	0.93
75	0.93	1.16	1.39
100	1.25	1.55	1.86
200	2.50	3.10	3.72
300	3.75	4.65	5.58

Making the Pour

1 Filling the Form. Plan the job before the truck arrives. Start pouring and spreading the concrete at the part of the form that is farthest from the truck.

Move the concrete with rakes and shovels. During the pour, fill all forms

1 Pull wet concrete to the back of the form.

to their top edges. Pay special attention to corners, along the edges of forms, or at any turns or curves in the forms. Spade the concrete in these areas. A rake is easier than a shovel because you can easily pull the material in place and then lift the rake out. You will have to use a shovel in some instances to lift material and move it back into odd areas.

Pour concrete in only one section at a time. When that is done, move to the next area while your helpers screed off the first section.

2 Screeding the Concrete. Select a straight 2x4. Sight along the edge of the board to see if there is any noticeable "crown." If there is, place the concave side against the concrete. A slight crown on your pour will provide additional drainage. The convex side would dish out the surface.

Starting at one end of the pour, move the screed toward the front to strike off the excess concrete as you go. Move the screed back and forth sideways in a sawing motion as you progress to help slide it through the excess. This action not only removes the excess but also pushes the larger pieces of aggregate down just below the surface of the pour. If you find low spots behind the screed in some

areas, use the shovel to move some of the excess concrete to fill these areas, then screed again.

3 Spading and Tamping the Concrete. Insert the shovel vertically into the concrete then pull the shovel up and down to remove the air pockets that may occur in the corners or along the sides of the forms. Be careful not to overdo this. Overworked concrete will separate—the water will break away from the cement paste and aggregate (sand and gravel) and float to the surface. Use the back of the shovel to press the concrete in place along the forms. Fill the forms to their top edges. Another way to eliminate air bubbles along the sides of the forms is to rap the forms sharply with your hammer, moving up and down the forms. This brings the cement paste out to the surface of the wall to cover the aggregate.

Tamping is similar to spading except that it is done over the entire pour. It removes most of the air bubbles and drives the large aggregate down in place so that they won't cause problems during the finishing process. Use a rake to jab aggregate down and work out any air bubbles. Be careful not to overwork the concrete at this step.

2 Move the screed in a sawing motion to strike off excess concrete and level the slab.

3 Gently tamp the concrete to push down rocks and remove air bubbles.

Finishing Concrete

There are several different types of finishes for concrete, and each requires its own set of skills and tools. This section focuses on the two finishes most suitable for the projects in this book. Both are easy to learn. These finishes can be accomplished by floating or by brushing with a stiff-bristled brush.

1 **Floating the Surface.** The first step in finishing is floating the surface of the concrete. This can be done with either a bull float or a darby. The bull float is used on large surfaces, such as patios and floor slabs. The float removes excess water from the surface and knocks down the small ridges left by the screeding operation. It leaves the pour smooth and level. The darby does the same thing, but is used for smaller surfaces or finishing off a slab after working the bull float.

Push and pull the large bull float back and forth over the concrete. At the end of each stroke, lift the float and move it to make another parallel stroke. When pushing it forward, tilt it a little so the front edge is raised; when pulling backward, tilt the back edge of the float so that it won't dig into the concrete.

After floating, cut the concrete away from the forms to a depth of 1 inch using a pointed mason's trowel.

2 **Cutting Edges and Joints.** Your concrete slab should be edged to create round, smoothed edges. Round edges are safer to walk on and look more professional. A round edge will also tend to chip less than a sharp edge.

Run a hand edger back and forth along the edge of the pour, holding the tool flat on the surface and against the inside of the wood form. Again, try not to dig the edger into the wet concrete.

If you have not installed permanent wood forms for the slab, then it will

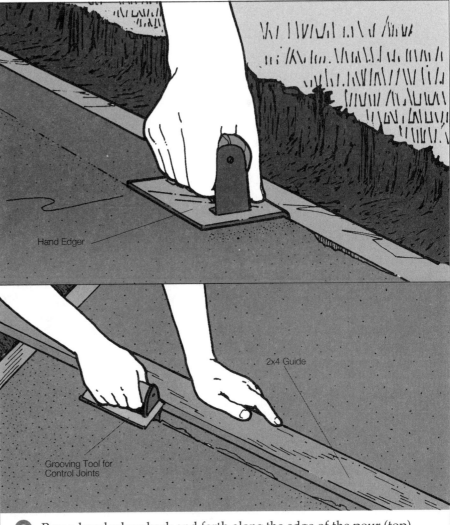

Bull Float

Darby

Hand Edger

Grooving Tool for Control Joints

2x4 Guide

1 Float large concrete surfaces with a bull float (top). A darby (bottom) is for floating smaller surfaces.

2 Run a hand edger back and forth along the edge of the pour (top). Cut control joints with a grooving tool (bottom).

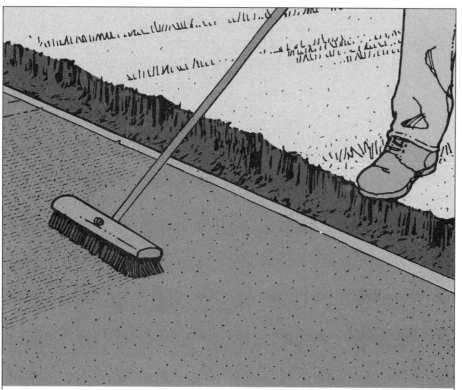

brush, because this may cause it to dig into the surface. For best results, broom the surface at right angles to the traffic pattern rather than in the same direction. You may have to touch up the edges and control joints with an edger after brooming the surface of the concrete.

Curing

Concrete continues to harden or cure for five to seven days after it is poured. Once you begin a concrete project, never allow the surface of the concrete to dry out completely. Mist the surface with water during the final finishing steps and begin curing immediately after final finishing.

The best and simplest method of keeping the slab moist is to hose it down at regular intervals or to set up sprinkling equipment. In all but the hottest climates, a good dousing at nightfall will keep the slab moist until the next morning.

The slab can also be sealed with plastic sheeting to keep in the moisture. Lay it flat and seal it completely at joints and along edges. Patch discoloration of the concrete can occur if the sheeting becomes wrinkled.

Form work can be removed a day after placing the concrete, but curing should continue for five to seven days.

3 Pull a broom toward you over the surface of the concrete for a textured finish.

be necessary to cut control joints every 8 to 10 feet. Cutting control joints is actually done in the same way but for different reasons. Besides providing a visual break in the expanse of a concrete slab, control joints provide a place for the slab to crack as it shifts and settles. Without control joints the cracks will be random and jagged.

Cut control joints with a grooving tool. Make the control joint one-quarter as deep as the thickness of the concrete slab. To provide a straight line, place the tool against a 2x4 guide strip tacked across the forms or a plank laid on the concrete. Work the hand groover along just like the edger. The V-shaped bottom will cut through the wet concrete to form the joint.

3 Making a Textured "Broomed" Finish. If you are pleased with the appearance at this point, you can choose to stop, or you may choose to try a "broomed" finish. A broomed finish is a bit rougher than a floated surface. The roughness provides

more traction so the slab will be less slippery to walk on when it is wet.

Brooming can be done with almost any stiff-bristle broom. Put the bristles down on the slab and pull the broom toward you. Lift the broom after each stroke. Don't push the

Timing the Finishing

If you start finishing the concrete too soon, you will bring too much water in the mix to the surface. Too much cement will be floated away and the result will be a weakened pour. On the other hand, if you wait too long, the concrete will set up so firmly that you will not be able to work with it at all.

Because of variations in humidity, climate, and even among concrete mixes, there is no way to say exactly how long you should wait. A good rule of thumb is to start the finishing process as soon as the sheen of excess water is gone and the concrete can withstand foot pressure. Another indication is the texture; the concrete surface should feel gritty under trowel pressure.

If you are using anchor bolts, remember to insert them before the concrete gets too hard. The concrete should be stiff enough to hold the bolt upright without tipping or sinking.

R O O F I N G

The roof of your gazebo is an important design element. The intimacy of the structure makes the roof a prominent feature. Whether you choose to use open slats, wood shakes, or composite shingles, the basics of roofing are explained.

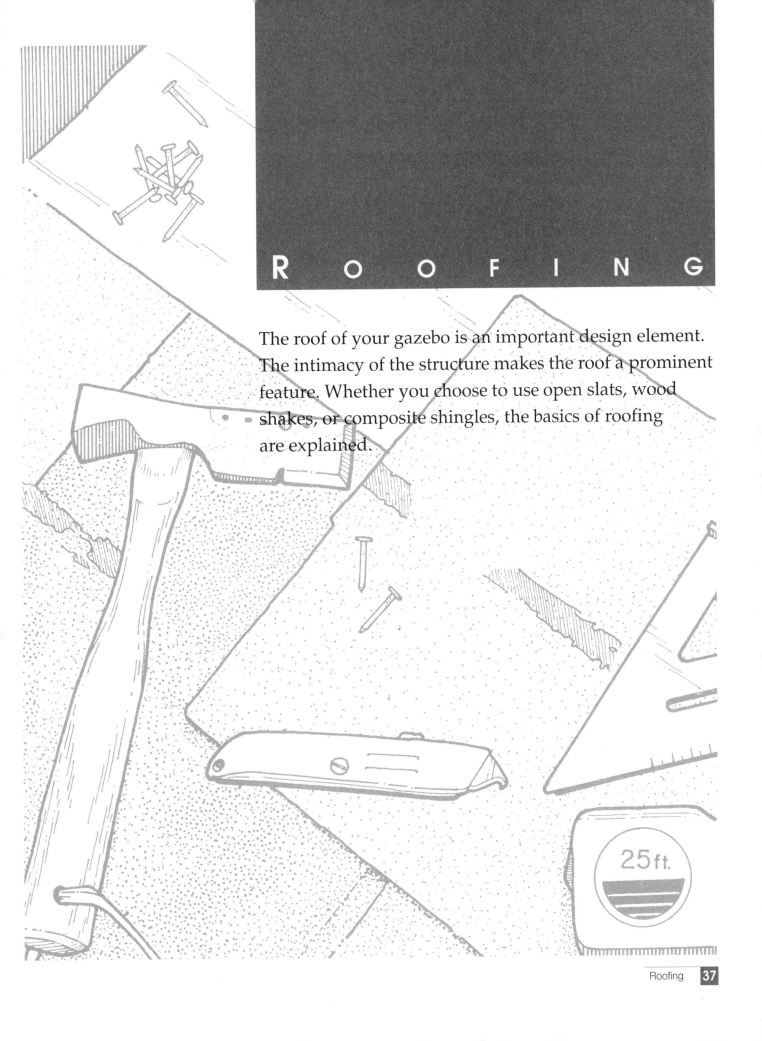

Choosing A Roof Style

When designing and building a roof for your gazebo, your priorities may be different from those you would have if you were building a roof for your house. For one thing, your house roof must be waterproof. That's not necessarily the case for a garden structure roof. Perhaps you want to roof your gazebo with lattice just to defuse the heat of the sun while admitting dappled light.

Another difference is that most house roofs are visible only if you step a good distance away from the house. Small visual details are less important than function. In comparison, the roof of your gazebo is much closer. And most gazebo roofs are steeply pitched, which adds to their visual impact. Your choice of materials will influence the style of your project; for example, standard square composite shingles provide a formal, practical structure; cedar shakes suggest a more natural feeling.

Perhaps cost would force you to roof your house with composite shingles, but when you consider the relatively small surface area of a gazebo roof, you'll discover that it won't cost that much more if you decide to spring for cedar shingles or shakes. Also, because the roof is small and easily accessible, you can take all the time you need to carefully craft roof details such as hips and peaks. A small project like this is a great opportunity to stretch your skills by trying new techniques and materials. This chapter will help you make the best possible choice by providing an overview of all your options and general installation instructions.

Wood Shakes & Shingles

It's hard to beat the traditional elegance of a wood roof. Cedar shingles and shakes have been used for centuries, not just for appearance's sake but also because they have proven themselves as perfect roofing materials that can withstand many years of abuse. Cedar naturally resists decay much longer than other woods.

Although wood shakes and shingles have several things in common, don't confuse the two. They are made differently. There are four types of shakes: taper split, hand split, resawn, and straight split. All but straight split are thick at the butt end and taper to a thin end. Straight split shakes are equally thick at both ends and are too bulky for most roofs. Tapered resawn shakes give a roof an even profile, because one face is smooth and flat. Shingles are sawn on both sides. They are smaller, thinner, and lighter than shakes and will create the most uniform appearance.

Wood shingles generally last 15 to 30 years, but shakes can last quite a bit longer, because they are split, rather than sawn from the wood. Wood's cellular structure consists of tiny pathways that carry water and minerals up the trunk to the leaves—similar to a bundle of straws. Splitting the wood along the grain leaves the straws intact so they remain open only at the ends of the face. Sawing slices into the straws creates lots of openings on the face that suck up moisture. Because of this, shakes are more resistant to damage from moisture changes than shingles.

Shingles and shakes are graded from 1 to 3 (with number 1 being the highest quality). Number 1 is used on most homes, because the shakes and shingles are cut from heartwood and are knot free. Lower-grade shingles (No. 2) are less expensive but

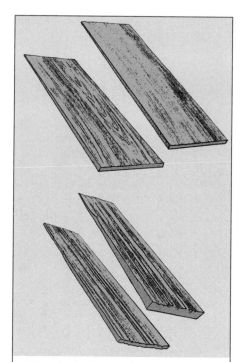

Wood Shakes and Shingles. Cedar shingles (top) are very different from cedar shakes (bottom)

are still more than adequate for use in a garden structure.

One obvious drawback of using a natural wood roof is that unless properly treated it's not fireproof. Shingles and shakes can be treated for fire resistance—some with a Class A rating—to fulfill most code requirements; however, this is an expensive option and may not be necessary. (This code may not apply for a garden structure; however, you still should check with your local building inspector just to make sure.)

Roofing Materials				
Type	Cost	Durability (years)	Sheathing	Install
Wood Shingles Wood Shakes	Moderate to Expensive	15–30 25–75	Slat Slat or Plywood	Moderate to Difficult
Composite	Inexpensive to Expensive	12–25	Plywood	Easy
Slat	Inexpensive	*	None	Easy
Lattice	Inexpensive	*	None	Easy

* These wood roof options should last about as long as the rest of the project. Durability depends on various factors, including the type of wood used; the type of finish or paint, if any; and the weather conditions the structure is exposed to.

Composite Shingles

Composite, or asphalt, shingles are available in a wide variety of colors, weights, tab sizes, textures, and edge configurations. The simplest shingles to apply and most common are the three-tab shingles, which measure 12 inches wide and 36 inches long.

The slotting is designed to give the appearance of a roof made up of smaller shingles. Also available are fiberglass shingles. They last longer than other shingles and have a Class A fire rating (other composite shingles are Class C), which makes fiberglass a better choice wherever there is a risk of fire.

Choosing Composite Shingles.

Composite shingles come in different weights from 215 to 390 lbs per square. The heavier the shingles, the more durable and more expensive. Thicker shingles can produce a roof with more texture. Some composite shingles are designed to mimic the random, rough-textured look of wood shakes.

There are dozens of manufacturers of asphalt and fiberglass shingles, and each calls its grades and styles by different names. However, the shingles are all basically made of the same material. Choosing between manufacturers is most often a matter of picking from what is available at the best price.

Storing Composite Shingles.

To prevent wind from lifting them, modern composite shingles are self-sealing. Strips of factory-applied roofing cement soften under the sun's heat to stick each shingle firmly to the course underneath. For this same reason, shingles should be stored in a cool location until they are to be installed.

Choosing Composite Shingles. Composite shingles are now available in hundreds of different colors. Some types are textured to mimic cedar shake or shingle roofs.

Storing Composite Shingles. Stack unused shingles out of direct sunlight. Excessive heat will cause them to stick together or bend out of shape.

Lattice-Style & Slat-Style Roofing

Lattice- and slat-style roofs cannot offer the same degree of protection as the other types, but their overall effect is hard to beat. These open-air roofs allow all of the summer breezes in while filtering out just the right amount of sunlight. They can also serve as a support for plants or flowering vines to grow on, so that your project can completely blend in to the rest of your garden.

Although lattice and slat roofs are a more custom option, they can be easier and less expensive to construct than roofing your project with shakes or shingles. For example, you essentially have to install a slat-style roof before you can start nailing on wooden shingles. By stopping at this step, you save yourself the money that you would have spent on the additional material.

Estimating Roofing Materials

Roofing material is sold by the square; 1 square is equal to 100 square feet. To estimate the amount of shingles you'll need, you must determine the number of squares in the roof's surface. The simplest way to do this is to climb up onto the roof and measure the area (length x width) of each surface, add those figures together, and divide the result by 100. Add 10 percent to allow for waste. Round up to the next highest figure. (At this point, it's better to overestimate what you will need. Unopened bundles can be returned, and since different pallets of the same shingle may have slightly different colors, you should order more than you need to finish the job on your first try.)

You will also have to include in your estimate certain specialty shingles. To approximate the number of hip and ridge shingles that you will need, measure the lengths of the hips and ridges, and divide the total by the exposure recommended for the shin-

gles. For example, the Eight-Sided Gazebo (page 68) has eight hips, each about 7½ feet long. The hips have a combined length of almost 60 feet, or 720 inches. Assuming that you want a 5-inch exposure, you would need 144 (720/5 = 144) hip shingles, or 48 regular shingles cut in threes. Don't forget to measure the total length of eaves and rakes for drip-edge flashing.

With wood shingles, 1 square will cover about 240 lineal feet of double course; 1 square of shakes will cover about 120 lineal feet. One bundle of factory-produced ridge units will cover 16⅔ lineal feet for both wood shingles and shakes. On shake roofs you must also figure about one and a half rolls of 30-lb felt, 18 inches wide, for each square of shakes at a 10-inch exposure.

For roofing nails, use 1½ lb per square of composite shingles and 2 lb per square of wood shingles or shakes. You'll also need about 3 lb

of nails for the starter course and the hip and ridge shingles.

Sheathing

Plywood Sheathing. This is a perfect base for composite shingles or for shakes. Use 3/4-inch exterior plywood, B-grade or better. Install the good side down, since you will be able to see it from inside your gazebo.

Run the panels perpendicular to the rafters. Use 8d hot-dipped galvanized nails every 6 inches along the ends and every 12 inches on the inside of each sheet. Leave 1/8-inch gaps at the edges to allow for expansion.

Using Texture 1-11. Texture 1-11 (T1-11) is a form of plywood made to resemble slat-style paneling. Typically, it is used for exterior siding, but in this case, it can also be used effectively for roof work. Install the T1-11 so that the slat pattern is facing down into the gazebo. Make sure

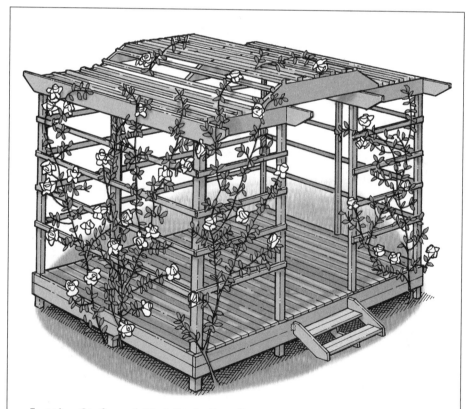

Lattice-Style and Slat-Style Roofing. A slat-style roof is perfect for filtering out the worst of the summer sun. For additional shade, plant climbing vines or flowers.

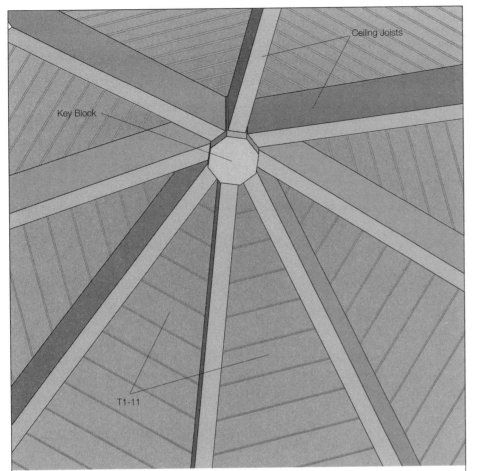

Using Texture 1-11. T1-11 used under a shake or composite roof can create a finished slat appearance, unlike ordinary plywood sheathing.

and set the third board on a 5-inch center from the second board. Now measure the space between the two boards and make a wooden gauge to space the rest of the sheathing. Solid-slat sheathing for the first 12 to 24 inches makes installing the first few courses much easier.

Many people prefer the open-air feeling of a slat-style roof. If you are concerned with letting in the sun more than keeping out the rain, you can stop right at this step. Obviously, you will not plan your slat width or slat spacing on shingle layout, but on the amount of light that you want inside your structure.

Felt Underlayment

Standard rolls of felt underlayment are 36 inches wide and 144 feet long. When used under asphalt or fiberglass shingles, plan on four standard rolls of 15-lb asphalt-saturated felt for every square of shingles. For a composite roof, lay each course of felt over the lower by at least 2 inches. Overlap each end by 4 inches. Lap the felt at least 6 inches over all hips and ridges.

that the sheets are positioned so that the slats are oriented in the same direction.

Sheathing & Roofing with Spaced Slats

Spaced slats are simply 1x4s or 1x6s, nailed directly to the rafters. They are used primarily with wood shingles and shakes, because these materials need air to circulate on both sides to prevent moisture from rotting or cupping the wood.

The measurement for spaced sheathing depends on the exposure of the shingles and is easy to figure out. Start with the second sheathing board—this is where the first row of shingles must be nailed. For example, if the roof exposure is to be 5 inches, set the second board right next to the first board. Next measure from the second sheathing board

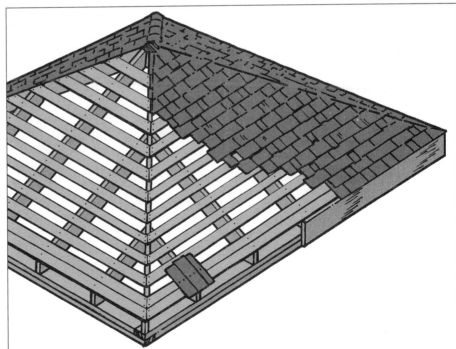

Sheathing and Roofing with Spaced Slats. Spaced slat sheathing allows wood roofs to dry quickly, preventing rot.

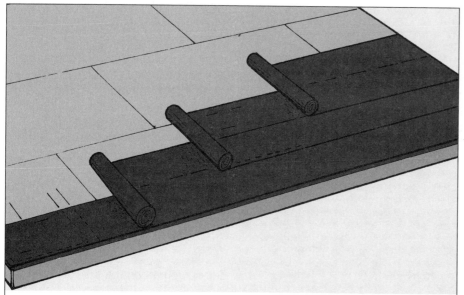

Felt Underlayment. The preferred underlayment for cedar shakes and composite shingles is 15-lb felt. Staple the felt in place.

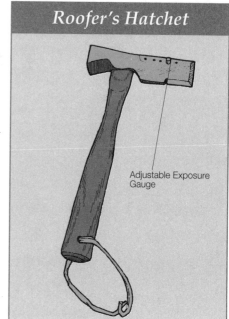

Adjustable Exposure Gauge

The roofer's hatchet is a specialized tool. It has a nonskid head, an adjustable pin for gauging shingle exposure, and a wrist strap to prevent it from falling off the roof.

Underlayment is used a little differently with cedar shakes. Shakes require 18-inch rolls instead of 36-inch rolls. The half-size rolls are "woven" between each course to ensure a watertight roof. Plan on using approximately one and a half rolls of felt for shakes at 10-inch exposure. If 18-inch rolls are not available, you can cut pieces from a 36-inch roll in half with a utility knife.

Installing Wood Shingles and Shakes

Wood shingles and shakes can be applied by anybody reasonably skilled with a few simple tools. This section will provide you with all the necessary fundamentals, but don't expect to be able to work at the rate of an accomplished wood shingler. Realistically, doing a job like this for the first time will demand some patience, but you will surprise yourself with professional-looking results.

Tools & Equipment

One tool that you will need is the roofer's hatchet. The hatchet has a nonskid head that prevents it from slipping off the rough galvanized nails and a blade for cutting and splitting shingles; the better hatchets also have an exposure gauge. The gauge is important for spacing wood shingles. A peg fits into the gauge holes and is used to set shingles quickly to the correct exposure. If you use a hatchet with a sliding gauge, be careful—if it slips slightly you'll wind up with misaligned shingles. You will also need a saw for cutting shingles across the grain and a block plane for beveling the edges so that you can ease in the shingles and clean up cuts.

Material Selection & Exposure

Proper application starts with selecting the right shingles for the job. A good wood shingle roof is never less than three layers thick. Consequently, the exposure of any given shingle must be slightly less than one-third its total length. The amount of shingle or shake exposed to the weather varies with the shingle's length and the roof's slope. Thinner wood shingles should be installed in a straight line like composite shingles. Thicker wood shakes, on the other hand, look great when installed in a more random pattern.

See the table "Recommended Exposures," but again, it's a good idea to check with your local building department.

Recommended Exposures

Shingle Size	3 in 12 Roof	4 in 12 and Steeper Roofs
16 inch	3¾ inches	5 inches
18 inch	4½ inches	5½ inches
24 inch	5¾ inches	7½ inches

Choosing the Right Nail. The nails are the next most important part of a wood shingle or shake roof. Use only rust-resistant nails, either zinc coated or aluminum. Figure a little over 2 lb per square for both shingles and shakes. Use 3d nails for 16- and 18-inch wood shingles and 4d for 24-inch wood shingles. Handsplit shakes require a 6d roofing nails. A rule of thumb is to make sure that the nail penetrates at least 1/2 inch into the sheathing.

Installing Wood Shingles

Do not use a felt underlayment with wood shingles. Nail them directly over spaced sheathing. Take a little extra time getting started—the rest of the roof will be gauged from your beginning course.

1 Laying Out the First Course.
Begin by nailing a shingle at each end of the eaves so that they overhang the eaves by 1 inch and the rake by 1/4 to 3/8 inch. Drive a nail into the butt of each shingle and stretch a line between them to help align the rest of the starter course.

Right handers normally start in the left corner and apply enough shingles so that they are able to sit down on the roof. If you're a lefty, start on the right corner.

2 Running the Course.
Leave a 1/8- to 1/4-inch gap between shingles. Double the first course of shingles, staggering gaps by at least 1½ inches.

3 Starting the Second Course.
Start the second course of shingles at the recommended exposure. Proper positioning of the nails is very important. Two nails are required per shingle, regardless of width, to prevent the shingle from cupping. Always nail within 3/4 inch (1 inch for shakes) of the side edge of the shingle. Nail high enough so that the nails will be covered by the next course. On wood shingles with a 5-inch exposure, nail about 7 inches from the bottom edge of the shingle. On shingles with a 10-inch exposure, nail about 12 inches from the bottom edge. If you nail too high or too far in from the edge, the shingles will be able to curl up.

To locate the correct placement for each nail, measure up from the butt of the shingle you are nailing a distance equal to the exposure plus 1 or 2 inches. For a quick guide, mark the handle of your hammer with tape or a notch. Nail carefully; pounding too hard can break the wood fibers. If a shingle is crooked, pull it out and replace it.

Stagger gaps between shingles at least 1½ inches between courses. Gaps should not line up over gaps two courses below.

If the shingle splits while you are nailing it and the crack offsets the joint in the shingle below by at least 1½ inches, place a nail on each side of the split. You can treat the split

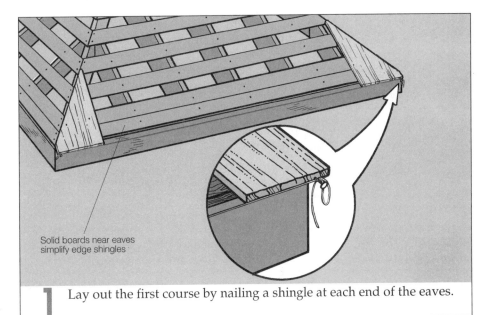

Solid boards near eaves simplify edge shingles

1 Lay out the first course by nailing a shingle at each end of the eaves.

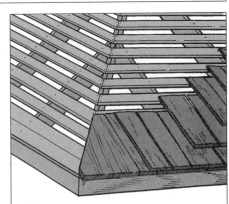

2 Double the first course of shingles with staggered gaps of 1½ in.

shingle as two shingles. If the crack does not offset the joint in the shingle below, remove the split shingle and apply another.

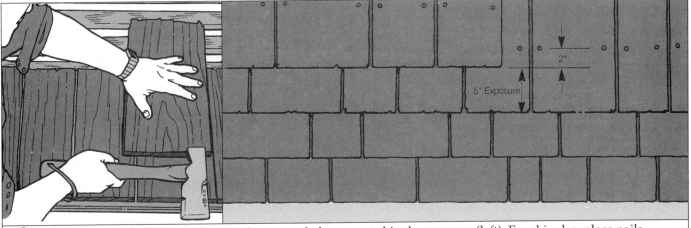

3 Hook the exposure gauge pin over the course below to set shingle exposure (left). For shingles, place nails 3/4 in. from the edge of the shingles, and 2 in. higher than the exposure height (right).

5" Exposure

2"

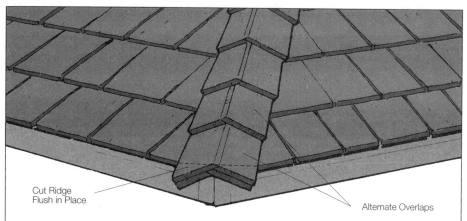

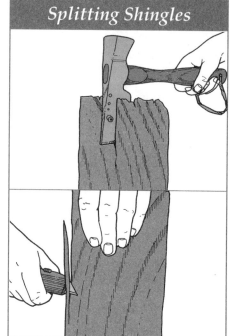

Cut Ridge
Flush in Place

Alternate Overlaps

Shingling the Ridge. Alternating overlaps ensure that water cannot run through hip and ridge shingles. Double the first course of each run.

Splitting Shingles

Because of their pronounced grain, shingles are surprisingly easy to split accurately along the grain. To split a shingle to width, embed the blade of a roofer's hatchet into the tapered end of the shingle then strike down. To fine-tune a cut, shave the shingle with a utility knife.

Shingling the Ridge

You will not have to deal with valleys with any of the projects in this book, but you will have to know how to roof a ridge. The gazebos in this book all have hips, which are treated just like ridges. The appearance of your project (and its ability to shed water) depends on the neatness of the ridge. Factory ridge units are available and will make the job easier, because the two pieces are already fastened together and offset mitered joints are stacked alternately to speed installation. However, it's not too difficult to cut the ridges yourself.

Cutting Your Own Ridge & Hip Shingles

Set your table saw's blade to a 35-degree angle and the fence to 4 inches (this measurement may vary according to the roof pitch). Cut two shingles at a time—one butt first, the other tail first. The top piece of ridge will come out about 1/4 to 3/8 inch wider than the bottom piece. The next piece will be reversed, giving you the same alternating mitered joints as the factory-made ridge pieces. For the next set, flip the pair (if the first pair was cut with top shingle tail first, make the second ridge unit with the top shingle butt first).

Each ridge unit must have two nails on each side, placed 6 to 7 inches above the butt edge. Make sure that you offset ridge joints so that water

will not seep through the joints as the roof ages. Give each ridge the same exposure as the roof shingles. For additional protection, it wouldn't hurt to lay a narrow strip of 30-lb felt over the ridge before installing the shingles. And always use a chalkline to make sure that the lines remain straight.

When starting a ridge run, start with a double course, as you did with the regular shingle courses. At those spots where the ridge meets the peak, you may have to trim the shingles to make a tight fit. Make the ridge in the middle and build a saddle by reversing two units on top of each other. Trim back the tail ends and leave about 8 inches of the butt

portion. Use longer nails to apply the ridge to ensure that the nails penetrate the sheathing.

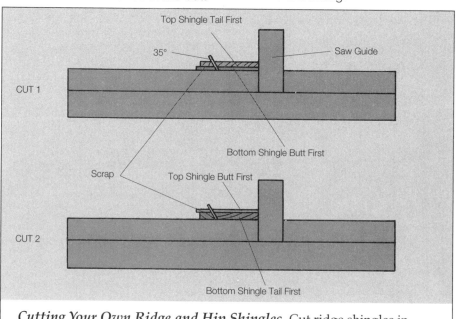

Top Shingle Tail First

35°   Saw Guide

CUT 1

Bottom Shingle Butt First

Scrap   Top Shingle Butt First

CUT 2

Bottom Shingle Tail First

Cutting Your Own Ridge and Hip Shingles. Cut ridge shingles in pairs, as shown, to create the alternating miter joints.

Applying Roof Shakes

Shakes work best on roofs with at least a 6 in 12 slope, particularly in wet, humid climates. Shakes measuring 18 inches are overlapped 10½ inches, leaving an exposure of 7½ inches. Shakes measuring 24 inches are overlapped 14 inches, exposing 10 inches. This amount of overlapping provides standard two-ply coverage. You can get even better coverage by using a three-ply roof; in this case you need a 12½-inch and 16½-inch overlap, respectively. Nail shakes with 6d box nails in the same way as you would for wood shingles, allowing 1/2 inch of space between shakes.

Preparing the Roof for Shakes

Shakes are usually installed over spaced sheathing, either 1x4s or 1x6s. However, because shakes are irregularly shaped, enough air can still circulate under them, even when using a solid plywood sheathing so that neither rotting nor cupping is a problem. If you decide to use plywood sheathing, you should not use any felt underlayment. The extra layer of underlayment will create a condensation problem; moisture under the shakes will affect your roof's life expectancy.

Except for a few minor considerations, shakes are installed exactly like shingles. When used to roof homes, wood shingles require 18-inch-wide strips of 30-lb roofing felt interwoven between the courses of shakes.

This underlayment ensures that any water that penetrates under the shakes will quickly be carried back out to the roof surface. If you want a completely watertight roof and cannot locate 18-inch-wide felt in your area, cut a 36-inch-wide roll in half with a utility knife. Either apply the felt as you install each course of shakes or felt only the area you plan to install in a single day.

There is a disadvantage to using felt in this particular application: Those black felt strips will be visible from the underside of your gazebo. You can choose to omit the felt entirely, but you may have to put up with a few leaks.

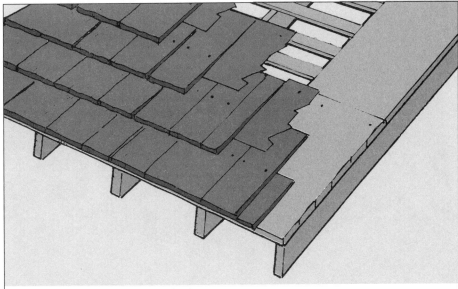

Preparing the Roof for Shakes. Shakes are applied over 1x4 or 1x6 spaced sheathing.

Applying Hip & Ridge Shakes

Cut and fit shakes at hip lines so that they end at the center of the hip. Shakes for covering hips and ridges are made with mitered edges. They require 8d nails or longer. Position shakes at the bottom and top of the hip and snap a chalk line between them along one edge to serve as a guide. Apply a double hip shake at the eaves, cutting the first one so that its top edge butts against the next course of shakes. Proceed up the hip, alternating the overlaps of the mitered corners.

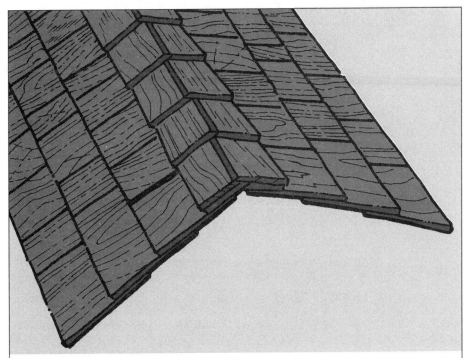

Applying Hip and Ridge Shakes. Ridge and hip shakes are mitered and applied with alternating overlaps.

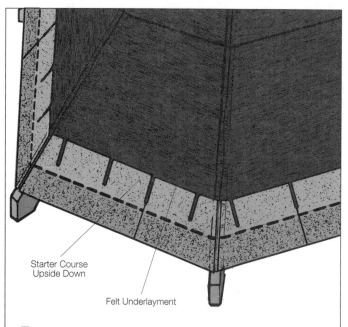

Starter Course
Upside Down

Felt Underlayment

1 To begin shingling, attach a starter course of three-tab shingles upside down on the felt underlayment.

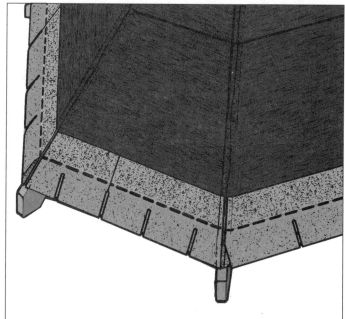

2 Apply the next row directly over the starter strip. Cover all starter course gaps.

Applying Composite Shingles

1 Installing the Starter Course.
After installing the felt underlayment and metal drip edge, begin with a row of solid roofing along an eaves, using either starter-strip material or three-tab shingles turned upside down. Snap a chalk line to keep the top edges straight. Overlap the starter course 3/8 inch beyond the edge of the roof.

2 Installing the Course Rows.
Next apply the first row directly on top of the starter strip. Make sure the ends do not line up over the gaps below. Work from one end toward the other as far as you can reach, then begin the next course without changing your position. Start as many courses as you can reach before moving.

3 Maintaining Consistent Spacing. The weather exposure for composition shingles is 5 inches. Keep the courses from drifting out of line by measuring up from the eaves at several points along the course being applied. Stop and check your progress from the ground to make sure your lines remain straight.

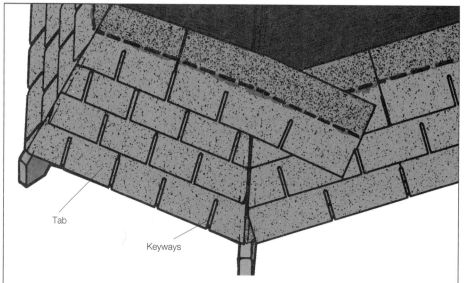

Tab

Keyways

3 Measure up from the eaves to ensure consistent spacing and overlap the shingles at ridges.

Nail each three-tab shingle using four nails, each about 3/4 inch above the top of the keyways.

When working on a six- or eight-sided gazebo, concentrate on installing the shingles in rows parallel to the bottoms of each panel. On the ridges that separate the panels, overlap the shingles. Cut them away in place. The ridge caps will cover up this unsightly overlap.

How to Cut Shingles

You'll save a lot of wear and tear on your knife by cutting asphalt and fiberglass shingles from the back. Use your knife to mark the top and bottom edges of the shingle, from the front. Flip the shingle over and cut through the marks. Save the larger pieces for use on the opposite rake.

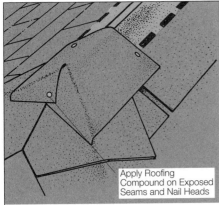

Apply Roofing
Compound on Exposed
Seams and Nail Heads

4 Fasten ridge shingles with one nail on each side of the ridge.

4 Installing Ridge Shingles.
Install the ridge shingles with the same amount of exposure. Fasten these shingles to the roof with two nails, one on each side of the ridge. Where the shingles meet the key block, fill the seam and cover the remaining exposed nail heads with roofing compound.

Applying Hip & Ridge Composite Shingles

Although hip and ridge shingles can be bought, it is easy to cut the required 12-inch squares from standard shingles, using a utility knife. To shingle a hip, begin with a double layer of shingles at the bottom and work up to the peak. Leave a 5-inch exposure. Nail 1 inch in from the edge just below the self-sealing strip.

When shingling a ridge, begin at the end opposite from the prevailing wind. Apply roofing in the same way as hip shingles, caulking the exposed nail heads of the last shingle.

Lattice Roof Installation

Installing a lattice roof is more akin to installing trim than to any of the other roofing options. The lattice roof offers little in the way of structural strength; subsequently, special care should be taken during installation... you just can't climb on top to set the last screw.

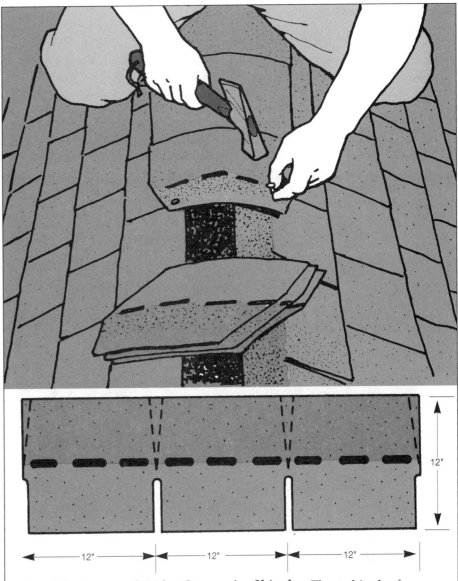

Applying Hip and Ridge Composite Shingles. Three shingles for use on a hip or ridge can easily be cut from one three-tab shingle.

1 Installing the Bottom Cleats.
Rip 1-inch strips off a piece of 1-by stock and fasten them on both sides of the opening that you plan to install lattice in. Nail or screw the cleat 1¾ inches down from the top of the rafter.

It's not necessary to surround the lattice completely on all four sides. The lattice will not have any load resting on it, nor are the spans in the projects in this book that great to justify the extra support. On the Six- and Eight-Sided Gazebos, for example, there's no need to worry about cleating around the point. Leaving the base open emphasizes the stepped pattern of the lattice.

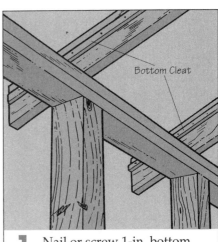

Bottom Cleat

1 Nail or screw 1-in. bottom cleats 1¾ in. from the top of the rafters.

2 Measuring and Cutting the Lattice.

Measure each opening individually, just in case they differ. Mark the measurements on each piece of lattice. Use a chalk line to ensure straight cut lines.

When cutting the lattice, rest the entire panel on a scrap of plywood. Make a straight edge jig by screwing a narrow board to a wider board. Trim the wider board by running the base of your saw against the narrow board. Clamp the jig along the chalk line. Adjust the depth of your saw's blade so that it cuts through the lattice and just barely scores the plywood underneath. Install each cut panel on top of the backing cleats, and tack them in with a few brads.

3 Installing the Top Cleat.

Cut the top cleat out of 1-by stock just as you did for the bottom cleat. Nail this cleat in to secure the panel.

Finishing & Maintenance

Red cedar does not need any finishing or preservatives under ordinary weather conditions. It will weather naturally to a silver-gray color. Over a long period, it will become almost black. In year-round warm, humid areas such as the U.S. Southeast, or in any site below overhanging trees, you should use a fungicide to control mildew and fungus growth. Some shingles may come pretreated; you can also apply a wood preservative and water repellent after installation. Wood shingles and shakes may also be colored. Use a penetrating wood stain—not paint—for this job. (Paint will seal the shingles or shakes so moisture can't escape.) Composite shingles require no special attention.

Clean wood roofs periodically to remove accumulated debris and to prevent moisture buildup. Use a stiff broom or brush to keep the joints clear between the shingles.

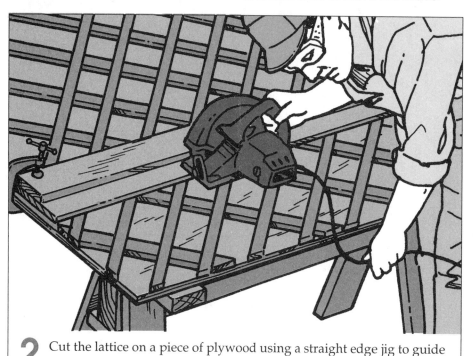

2 Cut the lattice on a piece of plywood using a straight edge jig to guide a circular saw.

3 Secure the lattice with a top cleat of 1-by stock.

GAZEBO PLANS

Now that you've learned all the basics of building a gazebo, it's time to get to work. The Square Hip Roof Gazebo, the Six-Sided Gazebo, and the Eight-Sided Gazebo each offer distinctive pleasures and different construction challenges.

Square Hip Roof Gazebo

This basic gazebo plan offers many advantages. First of all, it is square, so the need for the many special-angle cuts that you would find with six- or eight-sided gazebos are eliminated. The 8-foot-square design is modular, so standard-length lumber can be used with a minimum of cutting.

The roof in this roof-over-deck design is supported by 4x4 posts. The deck size is 8 feet across with a deck-to-roof distance of 78 inches. These proportions create an intimate, cozy structure. (Read this entire chapter as well as "Roofing" before finalizing your design.)

Measure and cut stock as you work. Take the extra time and give yourself the opportunity to correct slight errors before they become big ones.

The basic structural components of the gazebo deck are 4x4 posts that

Square Hip Roof Gazebo. This plan provides a lovely gazebo but eliminates the need for special-angle cuts.

Cutting & Materials List

Name	Quantity	Size
Gazebo Deck Framing		
Posts (Roof Support)	7	4"x4"x8'
Posts (Rail)	2	4"x4"x54"
Beams	6	2"x8"x8'
Stringer and Intermediate Joists	4	2"x6"x93"
Header Joists	2	2"x6"x8'
Center Joist	1	2"x6"x89 ½"
Decking Cleats	8	2"x6"x5"
Decking Cleats (Middle)	2	2"x6"x6 ½"
Joist Headers	2	2"x6"x8'
Stair Stringers	3	2"x10"x30"
Stair Treads	4	5/4"x6"x33"
Decking	18	5/4"x6"x10'
Roof Framing		
Top and Cap Plates	8	2"x4"x89 ½"
Key Block	1	5½"x5½"x8"
Common Rafters	4	2"x6"x59"
Hip Rafters	4	2"x6"x74 ¼"
Long Hip Jacks	8	2"x6"x39 ¾"
Short Hip Jacks	8	2"x6"x20 ½"
Rafter Fascia	4	1"x8"x94 ½"
A/C Exterior Grade Plywood Sheathing	4	3/4"x4'x8'
15-lb Roofing Felt		100 sq. ft.
Metal Drip Edge	4	8' lengths

Name	Quantity	Size
Composite Shingles		100 sq. ft.
Composite Hip and Ridge Shingles		Needed to cover approx. 26'
Railing		
Rails	12	2"x4"x41 ¼"
Front Rails	4	2"x4"x20 ½"
Rail Cap Piece	2	1½"x5½"x5½"
	2	1½"x3½"x3½"
Balusters	48	2"x2"x30"
Nails & Fasteners		
Carriage Bolts	18	3/8"x8"
Nails		
16d Common		
12d Common		
10d Common		
8d Common		
10d Finishing		
Roofing		
Post Anchors	9	
Stair Angles	4	
Framing Angles	2	For stringers
Premixed Concrete		As required to set post & step footings below frost line

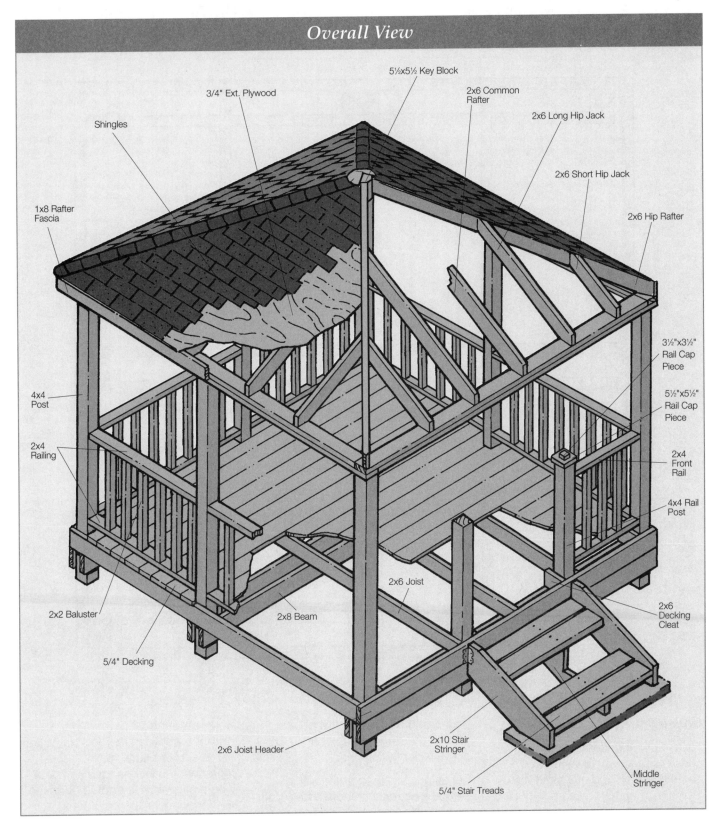

Shingles

3/4" Ext. Plywood

5½x5½ Key Block

2x6 Common Rafter

2x6 Long Hip Jack

2x6 Short Hip Jack

2x6 Hip Rafter

1x8 Rafter Fascia

3½"x3½" Rail Cap Piece

5½"x5½" Rail Cap Piece

4x4 Post

2x4 Railing

2x4 Front Rail

4x4 Rail Post

2x2 Baluster

2x6 Joist

2x6 Decking Cleat

2x8 Beam

5/4" Decking

2x6 Joist Header

2x10 Stair Stringer

Middle Stringer

5/4" Stair Treads

support the deck beams and roof headers; 2x8 beams that bolt to the posts and support the floor joists; and 2x6 joists, stringer joists, and joist headers that fasten to the beams and support the 1-inch-thick decking.

(Decking of this dimension is commonly known as 5/4-inch stock.) The gazebo must be square, level, and built to exact dimensions. Study the floor framing layout. All sides of the deck should measure 8 feet. The

corner posts are located 1½ inches inside the outside corners of the layout so that standard 8-foot lengths of lumber can be used for beams, joists, and decking. Note that accurate post placement is critical

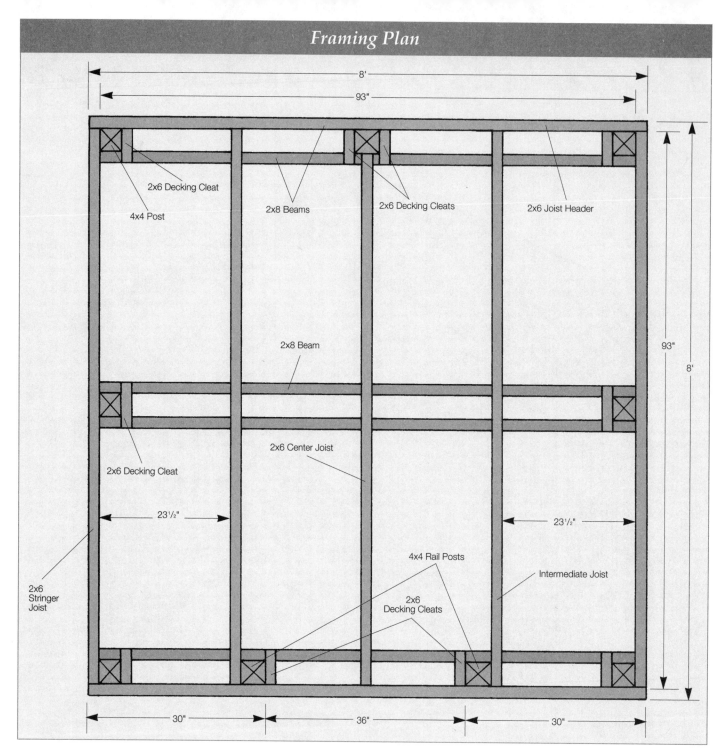

Constructing the Deck

To lay out the gazebo accurately, construct batter boards at each corner location and use the 3-4-5 layout method to locate each post (see "Laying Out the Site," page 29).

1 Installing the Posts. The seven posts that support the roof are 8 feet long. The two posts that terminate at railing height at the front of the gazebo are 54 inches long. These are not final dimensions. Final post sizing will be done when you finalize deck and roof heights later in the construction process.

Set all posts on concrete footings so that they rest on undisturbed soil beneath the frost line. The posts must be in their proper locations and exactly plumb for the floor and roof components to fit properly.

Place the nine concrete footings and metal post anchors, according to the instructions outlined in "Ground-work" on page 27. Remember, the distance between the outside edges of the corner posts must be no more than 93 inches. Use an 8-foot length of lumber to double-check for the required 1½-inch overhang at each corner as shown in the "Framing Plan."

2 Placing the Step Footing. Build a support for the bottom end of the step stringers by placing a 4-inch-thick concrete slab at the base of the step location. The slab measures 18x40 inches, with the front edge of the slab 26 inches out from the edge of the deck. Make the surface of the slab flush with the ground.

3 **Establishing Deck Height.** The finished deck is 16 inches above grade. This allows for a simple two-riser step design. It also keeps the framing members about 2 inches off

the ground. Mark this 16-inch height on one of the posts, and transfer this dimension to all other posts using a line level or carpenter's level. Once the deck height is marked, measure down 1 inch to find the height of the top of all joists. Measure down an additional 5½ inches to locate the top of the beams.

4 **Installing the Beams.** The beams are formed from two 8-foot 2x8 pieces through-bolted to the posts using two 8-inch-long, 3/8-inch-diameter machine or carriage bolts at each post location.

Temporarily tack-nail the beams to each post at the correct height, and check for level with a carpenter's level. Attach the remainder of the beams in the same manner, leveling them with the first beam. Then lay a straight 2x4, diagonally across the beams with a level on top, to check for level.

When all beams are tack-nailed in place and level, drill 3/8-inch-diameter holes through the beams and posts and install and tighten the bolts, washers, and nuts.

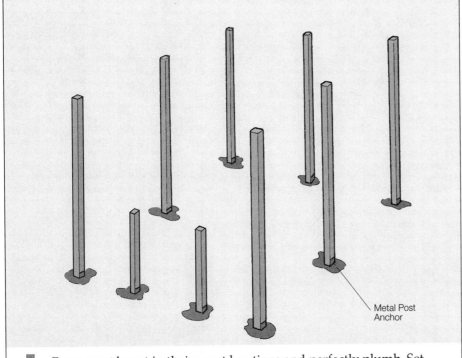

Metal Post Anchor

1 Posts must be set in their exact locations and perfectly plumb. Set in concrete footings or on metal anchors in concrete.

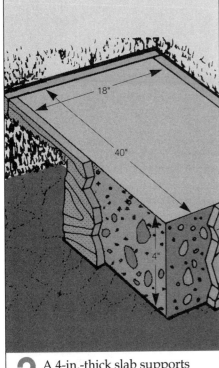

18"

40"

4"

2 A 4-in.-thick slab supports the bottom end of the stringers.

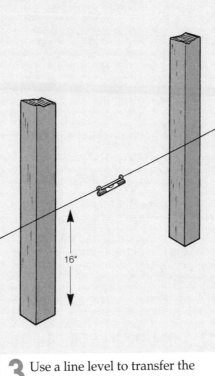

16"

3 Use a line level to transfer the height of the deck to all the posts.

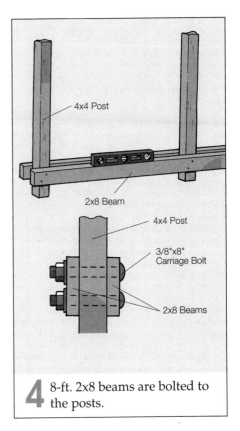

4x4 Post

2x8 Beam

4x4 Post

3/8"x8" Carriage Bolt

2x8 Beams

4 8-ft. 2x8 beams are bolted to the posts.

5 Installing the Joists. Rest the two stringer joists across the beams, against the outside of the posts. Fasten each of them to the posts with two 16d nails.

As shown in the "Framing Plan," one joist is centered across the deck, running from the front header joist to the back center post. Toe-nail each side of this joist to the back center post and to the beams with 8d nails.

Face-nail the two remaining joists to the front posts and toe-nail them to the beams.

Decking boards will have to be supported whenever they end at a post. Use ten 2x6 decking cleats to provide this support. Eight of these cleats are 5 inches long and rest on inside beams, ending flush to the outside of the posts. The two middle decking cleats are 6½ inches long and span the two middle beams. Attach the cleats to the posts with 16d nails. Predrill the cleats so they won't split.

6 Installing the Joist Headers. Use 16d nails to face-nail 8-foot 2x6 joist headers to the exposed ends of the joist at the front and rear of the gazebo. Nail the headers to the ends of the cleats and to the posts.

7 Laying Out the End Stringers. The gazebo uses a two-step "housed stringer" stair design. The 1-inch-thick stair treads are fastened between two 2x10 stringers. The connections between treads and stringers are made with a piece of hardware called a stair angle.

The stair has a rise of 5⅜ inches and a run of 11½ inches. To make the end stringers, start with two pieces of 2x10, each about 30 inches long. Place a framing square on a stringer as illustrated so that the 5⅜-inch mark on the outside of the square's tongue and the 11½-inch measurement on the outside of the square's blade both align with the top edge of the stringer.

Mark out the rise and the run. Extend the rise line to the bottom of the

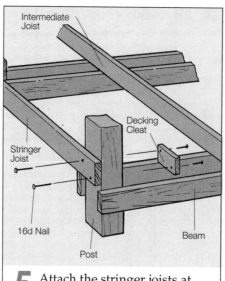

5 Attach the stringer joists at each side with two 16d nails at each post.

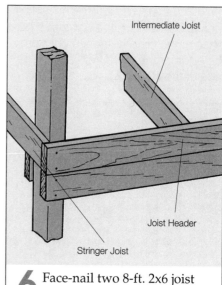

6 Face-nail two 8-ft. 2x6 joist headers to the exposed ends of the joists.

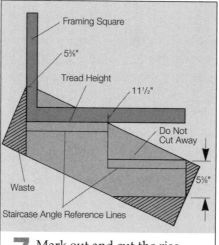

7 Mark out and cut the rise and run of the stairs on two 2x10 stair stringers.

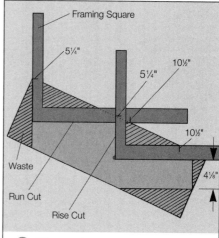

8 The middle stringer is recessed 1 in. behind the front end of the treads with a bottom rise of 4⅛ in.

stringer. You'll cut along this line to make the upper end of the stringer. Now move the square down to lay out the second step as shown in the drawing. Use the square to lay out the cuts for the front and bottom of the stringer. Measure down 1 inch from the top of the treads and draw layout lines for the stair angles. Lay out the other end stringer. Make cuts at the back, front, and bottom of the stringer.

8 Laying Out the Middle Stringer. You will have to include a middle stringer to support the 33-inch-wide tread. The middle stringer

is designed so that its risers will be recessed 1 inch behind the front end of the treads. As you did for the end stringers, use the framing square to lay out the rise and run cuts and the bottom cut. Note that the tongue of the square is now at 5¼ inches for the rise cuts while the blade of the square is at 10½ inches for the run cuts. Also, the bottom rise cut is 4⅛ inches for the middle stringer. You can do most of the cutting for the middle stringer with a circular saw. But you'll have to use a handsaw to finish the cuts where rises meet runs so they aren't overcut.

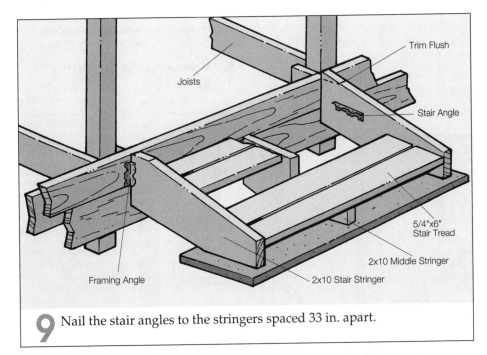

Labels in image: Joists, Trim Flush, Stair Angle, 5/4"x6" Stair Tread, 2x10 Middle Stringer, 2x10 Stair Stringer, Framing Angle

9 Nail the stair angles to the stringers spaced 33 in. apart.

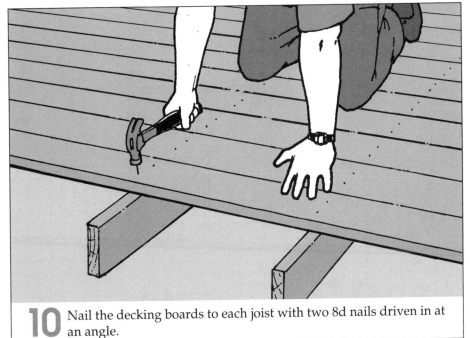

10 Nail the decking boards to each joist with two 8d nails driven in at an angle.

9 **Assembling the Stairs.** Nail the stair angles to the stringers with the nails recommended or provided by the manufacturer.

Use framing anchors to install the stringers to the joist header, spacing them 33 inches apart, equidistant from the rail posts. Nail the middle stringer to the front beam, centering it between the two outer stringers. When the bottom of the stringers sit flat on the concrete slab, the top points of the stringers should extend about 1 inch higher than the joist header. This is because the calculation for the rise and run of the stair included the 1-inch-thick decking. However, the decking will overhang the header slightly. To allow for this, use a handsaw to cut the top of the stringer flush with the header after the stringers are installed.

Each tread is made of two pieces of 5/4x6-inch decking. Cut the treads 33 inches long. Attach the front tread pieces flush to the front of the stringers. Leave 1/2 inch of space between the front and back treads. This will improve drainage on the steps.

10 **Installing the Decking.** Install the decking boards perpendicular to the floor joists, starting at the front of the gazebo and working toward the rear. Let the boards overhang the stringer joists. Later, you'll cut them all off even. For better appearance, align the first board so it overhangs the header by 1/2 inch. Several deck boards must be notched to fit around the posts. When cutting these notches, leave about 1/8 inch of clearance around the post. Both ends of each piece of decking must be supported, either by the joist headers, stringers, joists, or decking cleats.

Nail the decking to each joist with two 8d nails driven at a slight angle. You can use deck fastening clips instead of nails. Use a 10d nail as a gauge to space the deck boards.

After every three or four boards, measure to make sure the boards are running parallel to the back joist header. As you near the opposite end of the deck, note the remaining distance to the edge of the back joist header. It may be necessary to rip the last board to fit or to alter the spacing of the last few boards so you don't come up short at the end. Plan ahead by laying the last few deck boards in place before nailing them. Remember, you want the last board to overhang the back header by about 1/2 inch.

Snap chalk lines across the ends of the deck boards 1/2 inch from the outside faces of the stringer joists. If you have a steady hand and eye you can use a circular saw to cut freehand along the lines. Otherwise, tack a board to the deck as a guide for the saw. The posts will get in the way of the circular saw, so you'll have to cut a few boards off with a handsaw.

Framing the Roof

This square hip roof has four types of rafters, all made of 2x6 stock. As shown in the illustration there are four common rafters, four hip rafters, eight short hip jacks and eight long hip jacks. The rafters don't have bird's mouth cuts or tails that overhang the cap plate. Instead, they have a seat cut and a tail plumb cut that ends flush with the outside of the plates.

1 **Measuring and Cutting the Posts.** Measure up 78 inches

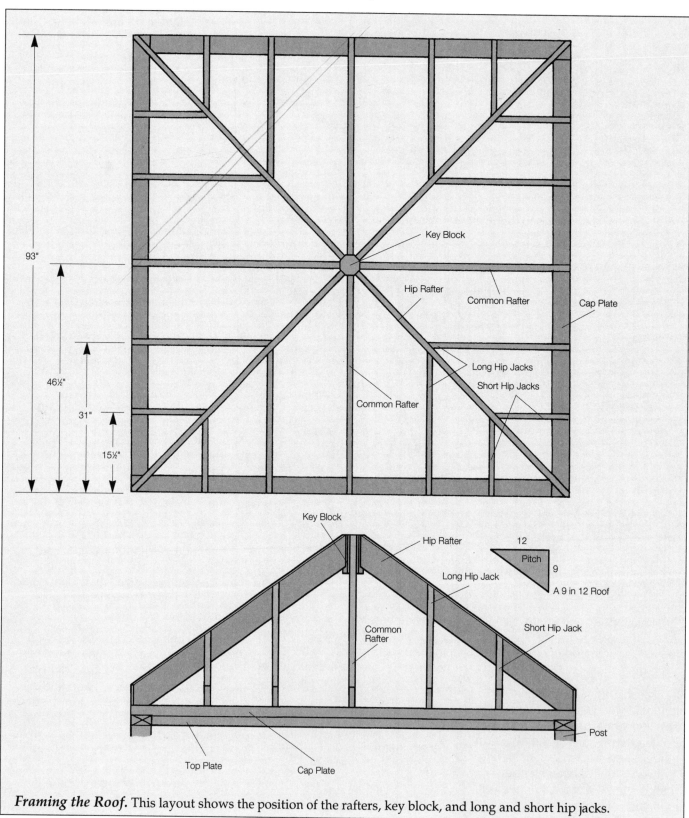

Key Block

Hip Rafter

Common Rafter

Cap Plate

Long Hip Jacks

Short Hip Jacks

Common Rafter

93"

46½"

31"

15½"

Key Block

Hip Rafter

Long Hip Jack

12
Pitch
9
A 9 in 12 Roof

Common Rafter

Short Hip Jack

Post

Top Plate

Cap Plate

Framing the Roof. This layout shows the position of the rafters, key block, and long and short hip jacks.

from the deck floor along one of the posts. Use a line level or a water level to transfer this height to the other posts. Mark and cut off the roof support posts at this height.

2 **Installing the Top Plates.** Cut the top plates and cap plates to form lap joints at the corners as shown. Nail cap plates to top plates with 8d nails. Nail one of these assemblies atop the front posts and another atop the back posts with 12d nails. Install the remaining two assemblies.

3 **Making the Key Block.** The key block will be at the peak of the gazebo roof. It has eight sides to meet the four common rafters and the four hip rafters.

Make the block on the table saw from an 8-inch piece of 6x6 stock. Set the table saw rip fence 3⅞ inches from the blade. Set the blade at 45 degrees and raise it to 2¾ inches. Now rip off the four corners to form the octagonal key block.

4 **Cutting the Common Rafters.** The common rafters and the hip jack rafters have a rise of 9 inches per 12 inches of run. The perimeter measures 93 inches by 93 inches, so make your rafters to the lengths given in the materials list. Use a framing square to lay out the tail plumb cut, the seat cut, and the peak cut as shown. To lay out the tail plumb cut, align the top edge of the rafter to the 9-inch mark on the inside of the framing square tongue. Align the 12-inch mark on the inside of the square's blade to the top edge of the rafter. Flip the square over as shown to lay out the peak plumb cut. Align the 9-inch mark on the outside of the tongue and the 12-inch mark on the outside of the blade with the top of the rafter. The seat cut is simply a line squared off the tail plumb cut line.

5 **Installing the Common Rafters.** Toe-nail two opposing common rafters to the key block with two 8d nails on each side of each rafter. Lay out where the rafters will land exactly

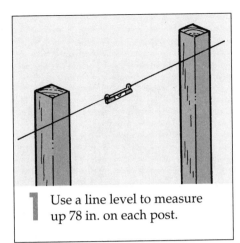

1 Use a line level to measure up 78 in. on each post.

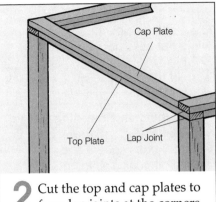

Cap Plate

Top Plate   Lap Joint

2 Cut the top and cap plates to form lap joints at the corners of the posts.

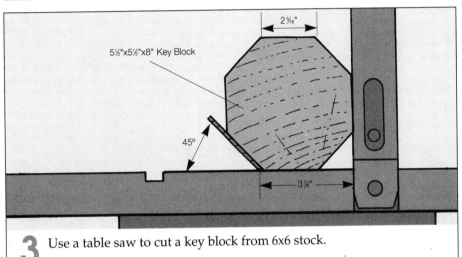

2 ⁵⁄₁₆"

5½"x5½"x8" Key Block

45°

3⅞"

3 Use a table saw to cut a key block from 6x6 stock.

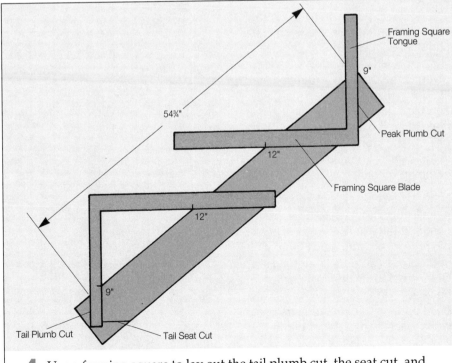

Framing Square Tongue

9"

Peak Plumb Cut

54¾"

12"

Framing Square Blade

12"

9"

Tail Plumb Cut   Tail Seat Cut

4 Use a framing square to lay out the tail plumb cut, the seat cut, and the peak cut.

on the middle of opposing cap plates. Now, with a helper or two, lift the two-rafter assembly onto the gazebo. Toe-nail it to the cap plates with 8d nails. Now install the two remaining common rafters.

6 **Cutting and Installing the Hip Rafters.** If you drew a box that was 12 inches square and then drew a diagonal line to opposing corners, the diagonal would be 17 inches long. Because of this, a gazebo whose common rafters have a rise of 9 inches per 12 inches of run will have hip rafters with a rise of 9 inches per 17 inches of run. The method of laying out the hip rafters, is the same as for common rafters except that you use the 17-inch mark on the framing square blade, as shown in the drawing, instead of the 12-inch mark.

Put the hip rafters in place, toe-nailing them to the plates and the key block. The rafters will overlap the corners of the cap plates slightly as shown. After the rafters are installed, use a handsaw to cut them off flush to the sides of the plates.

7 **Cutting and Installing the Hip Jacks.** The hip jacks have the same 9 in 12 pitch run as the common rafters. Their positions on the plates are shown in "Framing the Roof" (page 56). Their lengths are given in the drawing and materials list but measure between the plates and hip rafters before cutting to make sure the lengths are right. Lay out the plumb and seat cuts in the same way you did for the common rafters.

Make the tail plumb cut and the seat plumb cut just as you did for the common rafters. To make the peak plumb cut, set your saw blade at 45 degrees. Note that four long hip jacks and four short hip jacks are beveled to the left while the rest are beveled to the right. Toe-nail the hip jacks to the cap plate with 8d nails. Nail them through the bevel into the hip rafters with 10d nails.

5 Attach two common rafters to the key block on the ground, lift into position, and attach remaining common rafters.

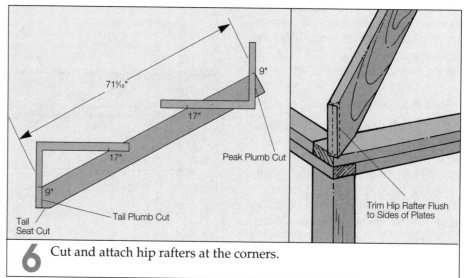

6 Cut and attach hip rafters at the corners.

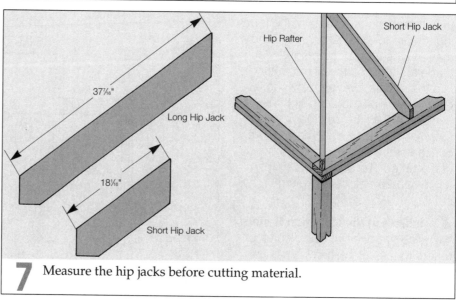

7 Measure the hip jacks before cutting material.

8 Installing the Rafter Fascia.

The 1x8 rafter fascia covers the ends of the rafters. Measure between the ends of hip rafters and cut the fascia to fit, mitering the ends. Attach the fascia to the ends of the rafters with 8d nails. Use a square as shown to keep the fascia boards low enough so that the plywood roof sheathing can go over it.

9 Installing the Roof Covering.

The roof is sheathed with 3/4-inch exterior grade plywood.

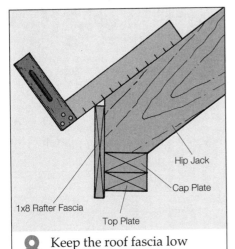

8 Keep the roof fascia low enough so sheathing can go over it.

1x8 Rafter Fascia
Top Plate
Hip Jack
Cap Plate

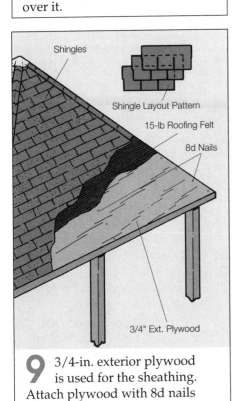

Shingles
Shingle Layout Pattern
15-lb Roofing Felt
8d Nails
3/4" Ext. Plywood

9 3/4-in. exterior plywood is used for the sheathing. Attach plywood with 8d nails every 8 in. on the rafters.

Each roof pitch requires two pieces of plywood—a trapezoid below a triangle. Cut the plywood to size and nail them to the rafters with 8d nails every 8 inches. Put the better side of the plywood facing down where it will be seen as the gazebo ceiling. Cover the sheathing with 15-lb roofing felt. Install an aluminum drip edge, and then install the composite shingles. Complete shingling instructions are given in "Roofing" on page 37. You'll also find instructions for alternative roof coverings such as wood shingles and shakes.

Installing the Railing

The two rail support posts can now be cut to their final height of 35 inches above the surface of the deck. Nail the cap pieces to the top of the posts, using 8d finishing nails.

Railing elements can be bought in most home centers and used to create many decorative possibilities. Trim these pieces to length and install between the 4x4 posts using railing hangers or by toe-nailing with 10d finishing nails.

You can build and install your own railing using 2x4 top and bottom rails with equally spaced 2x2 balusters.

Assembling the Railings

If you build your own rails, space the balusters as shown in the drawing. Lay out the top rail height at 33 inches above the deck. Measure and cut each top and bottom rail section separately to ensure a snug fit between the posts. Cut the balusters to 27 inches long.

Lay out the baluster positions on the rails, spacing them as shown in the drawings. Attach the balusters to the rails using 8d nails. Nail through the bottom rail into the balusters, but carefully toe-nail the top of the baluster to the top rail from the underside so there are no exposed nailheads on the top rail. Attach the assembled section to the post using railing hangers or by toe-nailing with 10d nails.

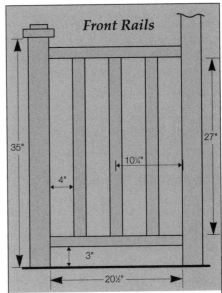

Installing the Railing. Cut the rail support posts to 35 in. above the deck and attach the rails and cap pieces.

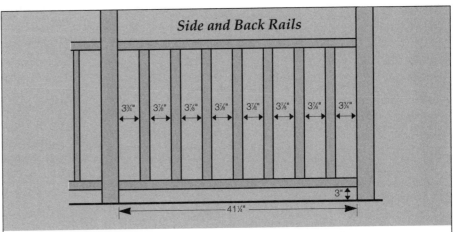

Assembling the Railings. Cut the balusters to 27 in. and space as shown above.

Six-Sided Gazebo

A six-sided gazebo is the classic design. It requires careful planning and accurate angle cutting, but for those with patience and skill, the results are well worth it. The deck of this gazebo measures 9 feet 6½ inches across, and the roof is constructed with a moderate overhang that extends beyond the sheltered area.

With six identical rafters, the roof of this gazebo is simpler to build than the roof on the Square Hip Roof Gazebo. You can make the roof framing even easier by using hardware specifically designed for attaching rafters on a six-sided gazebo.

You also can substitute a concrete deck for a raised wood deck foundation or add permanent benches or seating to your gazebo. We recommend that you measure and cut

Six-Sided Gazebo. This classic gazebo design requires careful planning and accurate cutting of the materials.

Cutting & Materials List

Name	Quantity	Size
Gazebo Deck Framing		
Posts	6	4"x4"x8'
Center Post	1	4"x4"x48"
Inner Rim Joists	6	2"x8"x52½"
Outer Rim Joists	6	2"x8"x54¼"
Diagonal Girder Support	2	2"x8"x cut to fit
Girders	2	2"x8"x8' 8½"
Center Beams	2	2"x8"x46$\frac{15}{16}$"
Inner Diagonals	4	2"x8"x11"
Outer Diagonals	4	2"x6"x12$\frac{5}{16}$"
Long Joists	4	2"x6"x47$\frac{5}{16}$"
Short Joists	4	2"x6"x34½"
Skirt Boards	5	1"x10"x59$\frac{1}{16}$"
Stair Stringers	3	2"x10"x30"
Stair Treads	4	5/4"x6"x 47½"
Center Hex	1	5/4"x6"x6"
Decking	24	5/4"x6"x10'
Roof Framing		
Headers	6	2"x4"x54¼"
Cap Plates	6	2"x4"x cut to fit
Key Block	1	6"x6"x8"
Rafters	6	2"x6"x81¾"
A/C Exterior Grade Plywood Sheathing	8	3/4"x4'x8'
15-lb Roofing Felt		100 sq. ft.
Composite Shingles		100 sq. ft.
Metal Drip Edge	3	10' lengths

Name	Quantity	Size
Composite Hip and Ridge Shingles		Needed to cover approximately 40'
Aluminum Cap	1	
Railing		
Railing	10	2"x4"x54¼"
Balusters	40	2"x2"x30"
Nails & Fasteners		
Nails		
20d Common		
16d Common		
10d Common		
8d Common		
Roofing		
Post Anchors	7	
Joist Hangers	4	Single 8" (for beams)
	16	Single 6" (for joists)
	2	Double 8" (for girder)
Roof-Peak Gazebo Ties	1 set	
Plate-Rafter Gazebo Ties	6	
Stair Angles	4	
Framing Angles	2	For stringers
Premixed Concrete		As required to set post & step footings below frost line

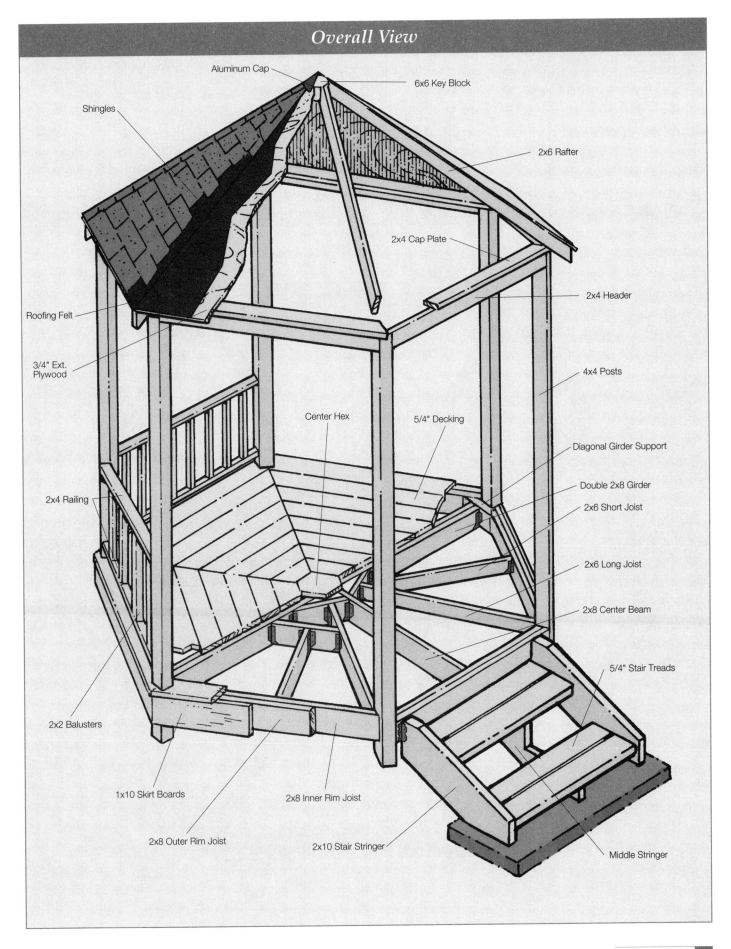

Aluminum Cap

6x6 Key Block

Shingles

2x6 Rafter

2x4 Cap Plate

2x4 Header

Roofing Felt

4x4 Posts

3/4" Ext. Plywood

Center Hex

5/4" Decking

Diagonal Girder Support

Double 2x8 Girder

2x6 Short Joist

2x4 Railing

2x6 Long Joist

2x8 Center Beam

5/4" Stair Treads

2x2 Balusters

1x10 Skirt Boards

2x8 Inner Rim Joist

2x8 Outer Rim Joist

2x10 Stair Stringer

Middle Stringer

stock as you work. The angles involved in most gazebo construction make precutting lumber risky, so take the extra time, and give yourself the opportunity to correct slight errors before they become big ones.

Constructing the Deck

Study the "Overall View" and the "Framing Plan" before beginning construction. The main support member or girder is made of two 2x8 pieces nailed together. Double 2x8 rim joists are used along with a network of 2x8 and 2x6 interior joists. Short diagonal pieces are installed between interior joists to create the 90-degree nailing angles needed to install joist hangers.

1 Laying Out the Post Locations.
Six posts support the roof at the perimeter of the gazebo. A single short post at the center of the deck helps support the main girder.

Before laying out the post locations, make certain the site is level. Select the center of the gazebo and drive a stake into the ground at this point.

Framing Plan

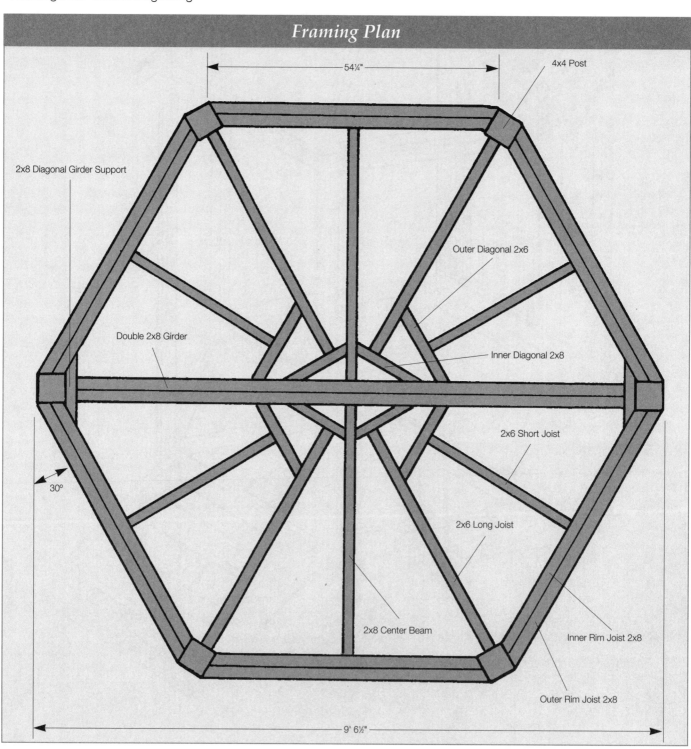

54¼"

4x4 Post

2x8 Diagonal Girder Support

Outer Diagonal 2x6

Double 2x8 Girder

Inner Diagonal 2x8

30°

2x6 Short Joist

2x6 Long Joist

2x8 Center Beam

Inner Rim Joist 2x8

Outer Rim Joist 2x8

9' 6½"

Drive a nail into the top of the stake letting the head protrude an inch or so. Cut a piece of straight lumber about 5 feet long and drill two holes 55½ inches on center. Fit one of the holes over the nail in the stake and then scribe a circle on the ground by rotating this measuring stick. You may wish to sprinkle sand along the scribe line to clearly mark the circle's circumference.

Now use the same measuring stick to lay out six equidistant points along the circle. Each point will be 55½ inches from its neighbors. These points locate the center of the posts. A second measuring stick is helpful in marking out anchor bolt locations.

2 Setting the Posts. All the posts are fastened to post anchors set in concrete footings. Use adjustable post anchors and fast-setting concrete to make this job easier. Dig holes for the footings at the center

and six perimeter locations. Pour the concrete footing in the center post hole and position the bolt for the adjustable post anchor.

Pour the footing for the first perimeter post. To position the anchor bolt accurately, slip the measuring stick over the center bolt and mark the 55½-inch distance on the concrete.

Continue placing the five remaining footings and anchor bolts around the circumference of the circle. Each anchor bolt will be 55½ inches from both the center anchor bolt and the adjacent anchor bolt. Remember, the posts must be in their proper locations and exactly plumb for the floor and roof components to fit properly.

After the concrete sets, slip the post base anchor over the bolt and install the washer and nut. The slot in the anchor makes it possible to adjust anchor location slightly and rotate the anchor to set the required 30-degree

angle between posts. When the concrete has cured and you are certain a post base is properly positioned, install the post on the base using the recommended size galvanized nails.

3 Placing the Step Footing. The steps can be located at any of the gazebo's six sides. Build a support for the bottom end of the stair stringers by placing a 4-inch-thick concrete slab at the base of the step location. Make the slab 18x54½ inches, with the front edge of the slab 26 inches out from the edge of the deck. This way, the slab will extend 2 inches farther than the sides and front of the steps. Make the surface of the slab flush with the ground.

4 Establishing the Deck Height. The finished deck will be 16 inches above grade. This allows for a simple two-riser step design. It also keeps framing members from contacting the ground. The deck boards are 1-inch thick (commonly referred to as 5/4-inch stock), so the top of the joists will be 15 inches from the ground. Mark this height on one of the posts and transfer this dimension to all other posts, using a line level.

5 Installing the Rim Joists. The inner and outer rim joists are made of 2x8 stock with 30-degree cuts on each end to meet the posts. If your posts are located properly and are exactly 3½ inches square, the inner rim joists should be 52½ inches long. The outer rim joists should be 54¼ inches long. But measure between posts before you cut the joists. Measure down 7¼ inches (the actual width of a 2x8) from the 15-inch marks on the posts, and mark the height of the bottom of the rim joists. Nail a temporary 2x4 cleat to each of the perimeter posts so the top of the cleats are on this layout line. Set the inner rim joists between the posts and rest them on the cleats. Rotate the post anchor to set the 30-degree angle and then tighten the anchor. Check the joists for level and tack them in position with a single 16d nail in each post. When all inner rim joists

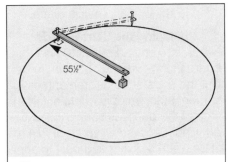

1 From the center point, scribe a circle with a 55½ in. radius. Mark off six points 55½ in. apart along the circumference.

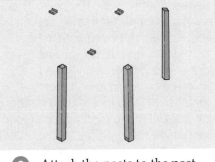

2 Attach the posts to the post base anchors. The posts must be set plumb.

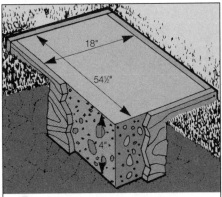

3 Pour a concrete footing for the base of the steps.

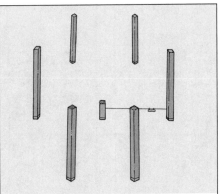

4 Transfer the height of the finished deck to all the posts using a line level.

are in place, check for level, and fasten each joist to the post using three 16d nails.

Once the inner rim joists are installed, size and angle cut the outer rim joists. Spike the inner and outer joists together with 10d nails every 12 inches.

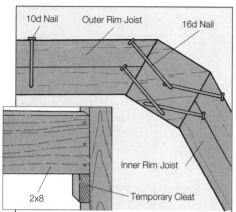

5 The rim joists meet the posts at 30-degree angles. Fasten inner and outer rim joists with three 16d nails at each post.

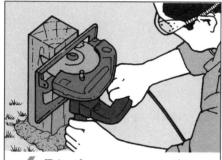

6 Trim the center post to the height of the bottom of the rim joist.

6 Trimming the Center Post.
Cut the center 4x4 post to final height using a portable circular saw. The top of the post is at the same height as the bottom of the rim joists and main girder beam.

7 Installing Floor Framing.
Because the main girder and the beams and joists that join it on an angle serve as a guide and nailing base for the decking, they must be positioned correctly. Measure as you go and use the dimensions given as a guide only. Center the joists and girder either on posts or on the exact center of rim joists as indicated.

Begin by installing the two diagonal girder support pieces that hold the hangers for the main girder. Cut 30-degree miters on each end of these pieces to meet the inner rim joists. Nail the diagonals to the posts and rim joists using 20d nails. Install the double hangers and then the girder. Spike the two 2x8 girder pieces together with 10d nails. Toenail the main girder to the center post. Locate the midpoint on the main girder and attach joist hangers for the two 2x8x46$\frac{15}{16}$-inch beams centered on this mark. Locate the center of the two inner rim joists that run parallel to the girder. Center joist hangers at these points for the other ends of the beams and install.

As shown in the "Framing Plan," the ends of all 2x6 joists are fixed on

short joists by hangers attached to diagonals. Install the four inner 2x8 diagonals between the girder and the beams. Make these diagonals 11 inches long with a 30-degree miter on one end to meet the girder and a 60-degree miter on the other end to meet the beam. Install 2x6 joist hangers on the post across from these 2x8 diagonals. Set one end of a 2x6 approximately 60 inches long in the hanger on the post, then move the other end until it centers on the midpoint of the main girder. Mark where the center of long joists fall on the diagonal and install hangers at these points. Cut these joists to length and install them into their hangers.

Cut and install the outer diagonals between the long joists and the girder. Make these diagonals 12$\frac{5}{16}$ inches long with 30-degree miters on both ends. Install hangers onto the centers of these diagonals and on the corresponding inner rim joist. Cut the short joists to fit and nail in place.

8 Installing the Skirt Boards.
Measure and cut 1x10 skirt boards to fit over the outer rim joists. Cut the ends at 30-degree angles to meet at the middle of the outside face of the posts as shown in the drawing. Cut a small scrap of 2x4 to fit between the skirt and post to serve as a nailer block. Don't use a skirt board between posts where the stairs will be installed.

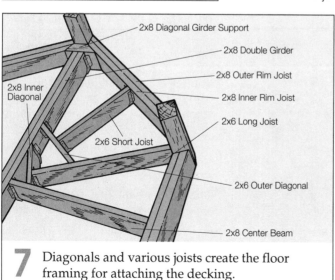

7 Diagonals and various joists create the floor framing for attaching the decking.

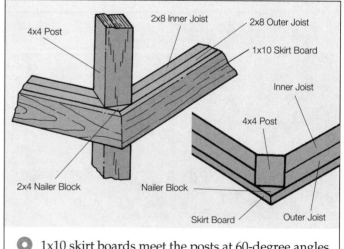

8 1x10 skirt boards meet the posts at 60-degree angles.

9 **Laying Out the End Stringers.** The gazebo uses a two-step "housed stringer" stair design. The 1-inch-thick stair treads are fastened between two 2x10 stringers. The connection between treads and stringers is made with a piece of hardware called a stair angle.

The stair has a rise of 5⅜ inches and a run of 11½ inches. To make the stringers, start with two pieces of 2x10, each about 30 inches long. Place a framing square on a stringer, as illustrated, so that the 5⅜-inch mark on the outside of the square's tongue and the 11½-inch measurement on the outside of the square's blade both align with the top edge of the stringer.

Mark out the rise and the run. Extend the rise line to the bottom of the stringer. You'll cut along this line to make the upper end of the stringer.

Now move the square down to lay out the second step, as shown. Use the square to lay out the cuts for the front and bottom of the stringer. Measure down 1 inch from the top of the treads and draw layout lines for the stair angles. Lay out the other end stringer.

10 **Laying Out the Middle Stringer.** You will have to include a middle stringer to support the 47½-inch-long tread. The middle stringer is designed so that its risers will be recessed 1 inch behind the front of the treads. As you did for the end stringers, use the framing square to lay out the rise and run cuts and the bottom cut. Note that the tongue of the square is now at 5¼ inches for the rise cut, while the blade of the square is at 10½ inches for the run cut. Also, the bottom rise cut is 4⅛ inches for the middle stringer. You can do most of the cutting for the middle stringer with a circular saw. But you'll have to use a hand-saw to finish the cuts where rises meet runs so they aren't overcut.

11 **Assembling the Stairs.** Nail the stair angles to the stringers with the nails recommended or provided by the manufacturer.

Use framing anchors to install the stringers, spacing them 47½ inches apart and equidistant from the ends of the outer rim joist. Nail the middle stringer to the front beam, centering it between the front 4x4 posts. Use two 16d nails driven through the inside face of the beam.

When the bottoms of the stringers sit flat on the concrete slab, the top point of the stringers should extend about 1 inch higher than the header joist. This is because the calculation for the rise and run of the stair included the 1-inch-thick decking. However, the decking will overhang the header slightly. To allow for this, use a handsaw to cut the top of the stringer flush with the header after you install the stringers.

Each tread is made of two pieces of 5/4x6-inch decking. Cut the treads to 47½ inches long. Attach the front tread pieces flush to the front of the stringers. Leave a 1/2-inch space between the front and back treads. This improves drainage on the steps.

12 **Installing the Decking.** Once the floor framing components are in place, the 1-inch-thick decking (commonly called 5/4-inch stock) can

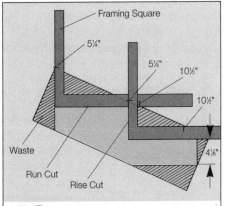

9 Cut the stair stringers from 2x10 stock with a 5⅜ in rise and a 11½ in run.

10 The middle stringer is cut 1 in. behind the front end of the treads. Bottom rise is 4⅛ in.

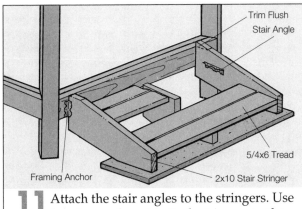

11 Attach the stair angles to the stringers. Use framing anchors to attach stringers to the outer rim joist.

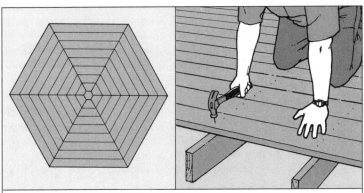

12 The decking design (left). Install 5/4-in. decking using a 10d nail as a spacing gauge (right).

be laid. Nail the decking to the joists with two 8d nails driven in at each joist location. Use a 10d nail as a gauge for spacing the deck boards.

Start by cutting a center hex piece from a 6x6-inch scrap of clear deck board. Strike chalk lines centered along the length of each joist that runs to a post. Make a mark on each line 2¾ inches from where they intersect at the center. Align the corners of the center hex with these marks.

Nail the center hex piece in place and use it as a guide to measure and cut the first row of decking. The first row then serves as a guide to cutting the second row and so on. End joints should fall along the chalk lines that run at angles from the center hex. A power miter box set for a 30-degree cut will speed this work.

Trim the last row of decking so it extends 3/4 inch or so beyond the skirt board. Since these are rip cuts, they'll be easiest to accomplish before the last boards are installed. You'll have to notch the last row of deck boards to fit around the posts.

Framing the Roof

The six-sided gazebo looks like it has hip rafters, but it really has six identical common rafters. This is because the rafters meet the posts at 90-degree angles. The rafters have a rise of 9 inches per 12 inches of run.

As mentioned, you can avoid bird's mouth and peak plumb cuts by using special peak and plate ties designed for roofs on six-sided gazebos. The instructions below explain how to frame the roof with and without this hardware.

1 **Cutting the Posts.** Mark one of the posts 78 inches from the deck floor. Use a line level or carpenter's level to transfer this height to the other five posts. Mark and cut the posts at this height.

2 **Installing Roof Headers.** Cut the 2x4 headers to the same length as you cut the outer rim joists, with

the same 30-degree angle on each end. Nail the headers to the posts with 10d nails. Make sure the tops of the headers are level with the post tops.

Note: If you will be using peak and plate ties, cut the cap plates now so that they meet each other over the posts with 30-degree miters on each end. Make sure the sides of the plates are flush with the faces of the headers. Nail the plates to the headers with 10d nails. The mitered corners of the plates will overlap the posts a little. You'll need to cut the ends flush with the posts to allow for the plate ties. If you will not be using plate and peak ties, do not cut or install the cap plates yet. You will install the cap plates after the rafters are in place.

3 **Making the Key Block.** The six-sided key block is used only if you are not using peak ties. Make the block on the table saw from an 8-inch-long piece of 6x6. Set the fence 2⅝ inches from the blade. Tilt the blade to 60 degrees. Rip the four corners off the block.

4 **Cutting the Rafters.** If you use peak and plate ties, the roof will be a few inches higher than if you don't, but the rafter length and tail plumb cuts will be the same either way. To lay out the tail plumb cuts, align the top edge of the rafter to the 9-inch mark on the inside of the framing square tongue. Align the 12-inch mark on the inside of the square's blade to the top edge of the rafter. That's all the layout you have to do if you are using ties.

If you are not using ties, slide the square up 12 inches to lay out the bird's mouth plumb cut. Now align out a 3½-inch seat cut perpendicular to the plumb cut as shown. Flip the square over as shown to lay out the peak plumb cut. Align the 9-inch mark on the outside of the tongue with the top of the rafter. Align the 12-inch mark on the outside of the blade and the 9-inch mark on the outside of the tongue with the top of the rafter. Cut the rafters to size.

1 Mark the posts 78 in. from the deck floor and transfer the mark to the other posts with a line level. Cut the posts at this height.

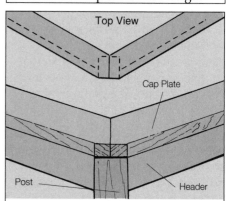

2 Install headers cut to the same dimensions as the outer rim joists. Install cap plates now if you're using plate and peak ties.

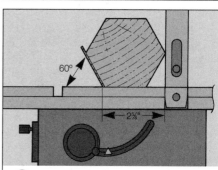

3 Cut the key block from 8-in.-long 6x6 stock.

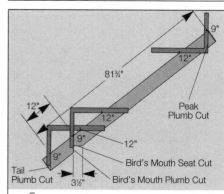

4 The rafter length and tail plumb cut is the same whether you use plate and peak ties or not.

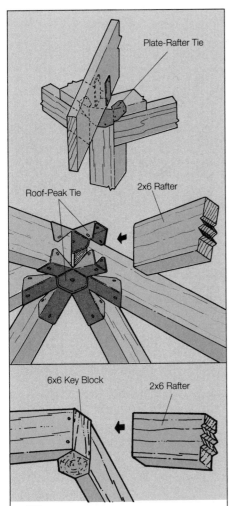

5 Attach the rafters to the peak and plate ties using the hardware recommended (top). Or attach rafters directly to a key block (bottom).

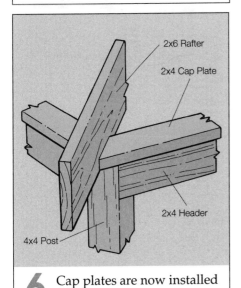

6 Cap plates are now installed between the rafters if no peak and plate ties are used.

5 Installing the Rafters. The plate ties are made to accommodate the gazebo's 60-degree angles. If you are using plate ties, simply nail them to the cap plates and posts as shown, using the nails provided or recommended by the manufacturer. The peak ties consist of a top and a bottom piece that hold the rafters as shown. Bend the legs of the roof-peak tie down to accommodate the roof pitch.

If you are not using ties, nail two opposing rafters to the key block. Then, with a helper or two, lift the assembly onto the header with the bird's mouths seated on top of opposing posts. Toe-nail the rafters to the posts with 8d nails. Assemble the remaining rafters.

6 Installing the Cap Plates. If you are not using ties, you will now install the cap plates. Measure and cut them with 30-degree angles at each end to fit snugly between rafters. Nail the cap plates to the headers with 10d nails. Use 8d nails to toe-nail the cap plates to the rafters.

Installing the Roof Covering

The plans shown here call for a 3/4-inch exterior-grade plywood roof covered with composite shingles. Cut the plywood triangles to size and install them over the rafters using 8d common nails spaced 12 inches apart. Complete the shingling. Instructions for installing wood shingles and shakes, composite shingles, and other roofing alternatives are given in "Roofing" on page 37.

Installing the Railing

You can build and install your own railing using 2x4 top and bottom rails with equally spaced 2x2 balusters. Lay out the top rail height 33 inches above the deck. Measure and cut each top and bottom rail section separately to ensure a snug fit between the posts. Cut the balusters to 27 inches long and spaced 5 inches on center. Miter the ends of the rails at 60 degrees to match the posts.

Attach the balusters (eight per section) to the rails. Nail through the bottom rail into the balusters, but carefully toe-nail the top of the balusters to the top rail from the underside so there are no exposed nailheads on the top rail. Attach the assembled section to the posts, using railing brackets, 2x4 cleats, or by toe-nailing with 10d nails.

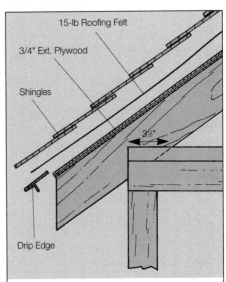

Installing the Roof Covering. 3/4-in. exterior-grade plywood is covered with composite shingles. Other roofing options are possible.

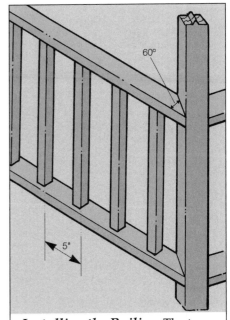

Installing the Railing. The top rail is placed 33 in. above the deck and balusters are spaced 5 in. apart.

Eight-Sided Gazebo

This eight-sided gazebo gets a special touch of elegance from its high, gracefully curved roof. The roof is created with curved rafters sheathed with slats. Of course you can simplify construction by using straight rafters instead.

Like the other gazebos in this book, this one is supported by 2x8 beams bolted to 4x4 posts. The beams support 2x6 rafters, which are covered with 1-inch decking boards. Decking of this dimension is commonly called 5/4-inch stock. The deck is 8 feet across. The distance from the deck to the top plate is 6 feet 6 inches. The materials list and drawings for this project provide specific lengths for the framing lumber. These lengths would be accurate if all

Eight-Sided Gazebo. The gently curved roof of this design makes for an elegant outdoor structure.

Cutting & Materials List

Name	Quantity	Size
Gazebo Deck Framing		
Roof Posts	8	4"x4"x10'
Long Beams	4	2"x8"x93"
Short Beams	2	2"x8"x45¾"
Square-End Rim Joists	4	2"x6"x42¾"
Decking Cleats	4	2"x6"x5"
Decking Cleats	4	2"x6"x4⅜"
Mitered Rim Joists	4	2"x6"x37¹¹⁄₁₆"
Long Joists	3	2"x6"x93"
Short Joists	2	2"x6"x51½"
Mid-Length Joists	2	2"x6"x78⅛"
Stair Stringers	3	2"x10"x30"
Stair Treads	4	5/4"x6"x32¾"
Newel Posts	2	4"x4"x41¼"
Stair Rails	4	2"x4"x24¾"
Large Newel Block	2	1½"x5½"x5½"
Small Newel Block	2	1½"x3½"x3½"
Stair Balusters	8	2"x2"x27⅝"
Decking	14	5/4"x6"x10'
Roof Framing		
Top Plates	4	2"x6"x39¾"
Top Plates	4	2"x6"x37¹¹⁄₁₆"
Ceiling Joists	2	2"x4"x8' 5⅛"
Ceiling Joists	2	2"x4"x49¹³⁄₁₆"
Ceiling Joists	2	2"x4"x49½"
Cap Plates	4	2"x6"x39¾"
Cap Plates	4	2"x6"x37¹¹⁄₁₆"
Key Block	1	5½"x5½"x12"
Rafters	8	2"x8"x8' 2⅝"

Name	Quantity	Size
Roof Slats	32	1"x4"x10'
15-lb Roofing Felt		100 sq. ft.
Metal Drip Edge	4	8' Lengths
Composite or Wood Shingles		100 sq. ft.
Composite Hip and Ridge Shingles		Needed to cover approximately 60'
Aluminum Cap	1	
Railing		
Square-End Rails	6	2"x4"x32¾"
Mitered Rails	8	2"x4"x37¹¹⁄₁₆"
Balusters	46	2"x2"x27"
Nails & Fasteners		
Metal Post Anchors	8	
Nails		
16d Common		
10d Common		
8d Common		
6d Common		
8d Galvanized Finishing		
Roofing		
Carriage Bolts	8	3/8"x8"
Lag Screws	8	3/8"x3"
3" Galvanized Decking Screws		
2½" Galvanized Decking Screws		
Stair Angles	4	
Framing Angles	2	For stringers
Premixed Cement		As required to set post & step footings below frost line

Aluminum Cap

5½x5½ Key Block

Shingles

1x4 Slats

2x4 Ceiling Joist

2x8 Rafter

2x4 Rail

4x4 Post

2x6 Cap Plate

2x2 Baluster

2x6 Top Plate

3½x3½ Newel Block

5½x5½ Newel Block

2x10 Stair Stringer

2x6 Rim Joist

5/4" Decking

2x8 Beams

2x6 Joist

5/4" Stair Tread

4x4 Newel Posts

2x10 Middle Stringer

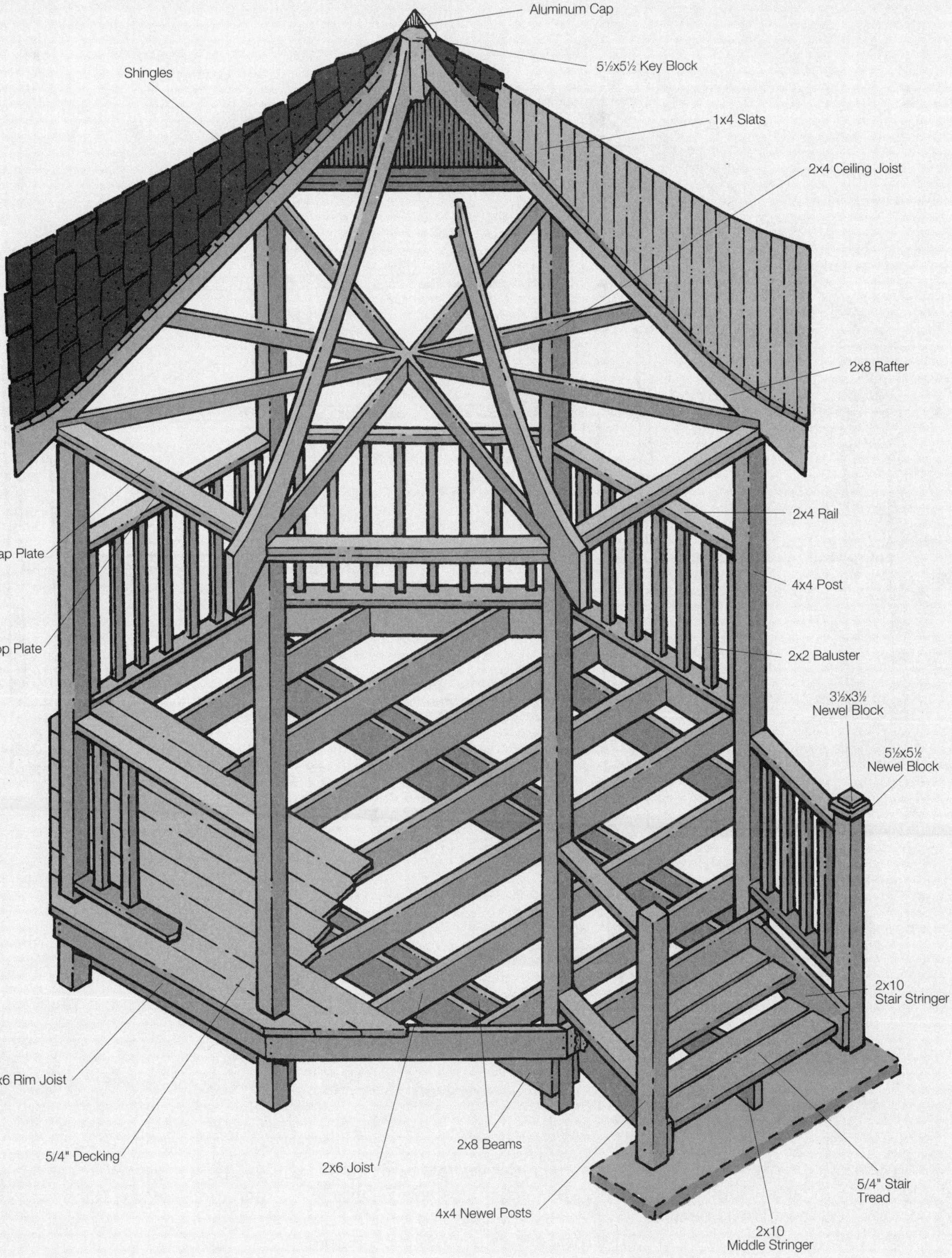

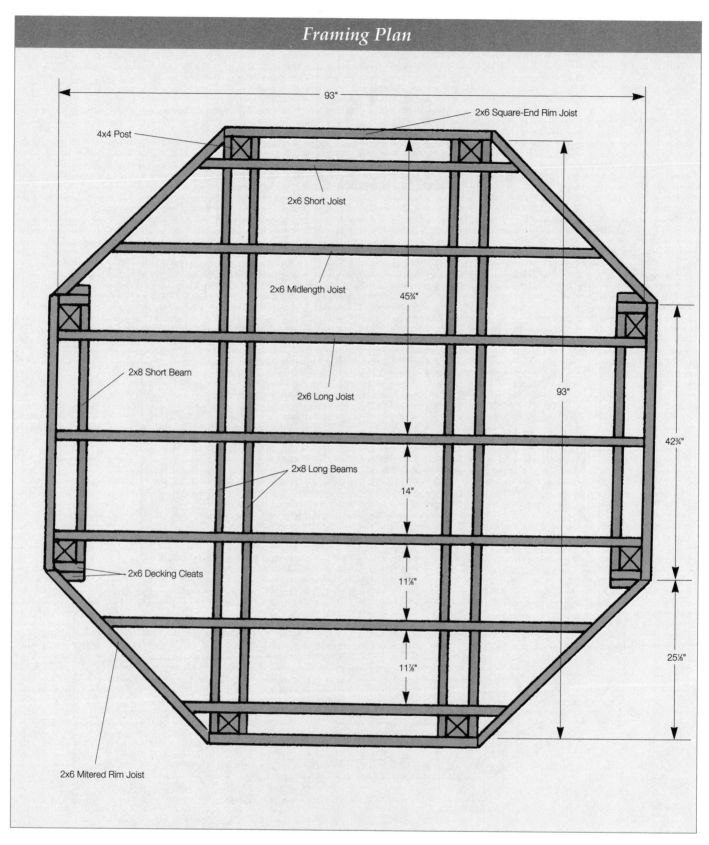

93"

2x6 Square-End Rim Joist

4x4 Post

2x6 Short Joist

2x6 Midlength Joist

45¾"

2x8 Short Beam

2x6 Long Joist

93"

42¾"

2x8 Long Beams

14"

2x6 Decking Cleats

11⅞"

25⅛"

11⅞"

2x6 Mitered Rim Joist

framing lumber were exact in width and thickness measurements, and if you managed to locate all posts and make all cuts with pinpoint accuracy. But the real world isn't like that. So measure as you go, adjust as necessary, and use the stated dimensions as a guide only. Before you begin, study the "Overall View" and the "Framing Plan."

Planning & Building the Deck

As with any project, careful planning and precise layout are essential, so take your time. This eight-sided building will require some fairly complex cutting and joinery; time invested now will eliminate the need to do any time-consuming alterations later.

Don't let the complexity of the octagonal shape discourage you. The layout and foundation work required for this project are basically the same as for the simpler projects.

1 **Laying Out the Posts.** Begin by constructing batter boards with strings to lay out a 93-inch square. See "Groundwork" on page 27 for instruction on how to set up batter boards. Use a felt-tipped pen to make a mark 26⅝ inches from each corner.

These marks locate the outside corners of the eight posts. From these points, locate the center of each post. This will be the center of your post holes.

2 **Setting the Posts.** The eight posts that support the roof are 10 feet long. However, this is not the final post length. You'll cut the posts to final height after you install the deck.

Set the posts on concrete footings that rest on undisturbed soil beneath the frost line. The posts must be in their proper locations and exactly plumb for the floor and roof components to fit properly. Place the eight concrete footing and metal post anchors according to the instructions in "Groundwork" on page 27.

3 **Placing the Step Footing.** Build a support for the bottom of the stair stringers and railing posts by placing a 4-inch-thick concrete slab at the base of the chosen step location. Make this slab 18x40 inches, with the front edge of the slab 26 inches from the outside rim joist. Make the surface of the slab flush with the ground.

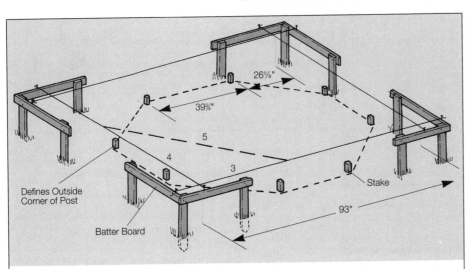

1 Use batter boards and the 3-4-5 method for laying out the corners of the gazebo. The outside corner of the posts are 26⅝ in. from the string corners.

2 Place 10-ft.-long posts on the metal post anchors.

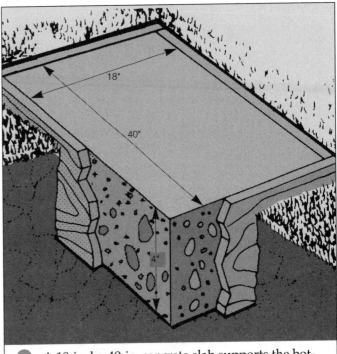

3 A 18-in. by 40-in. concrete slab supports the bottom of the steps.

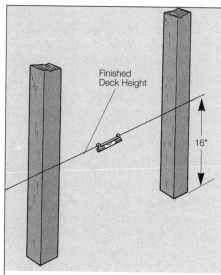

Finished
Deck Height

16"

4 Transfer the deck height of 16 in. to all the posts with a line level.

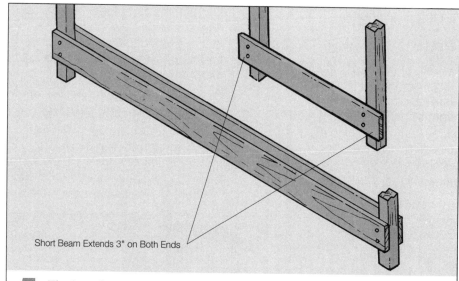

Short Beam Extends 3" on Both Ends

5 The long beams attach to the posts with carriage bolts and the short beams with lag screws.

4 Establishing the Deck Height. The finished deck height will be 16 inches above grade. This allows for a simple two-riser step design. Mark this 16-inch height on one of the posts and transfer this dimension to all other posts using a line level or water level. Once the deck height is marked, measure down 1 inch to allow for the thickness of the deck boards. This marks the top of the joists. Now measure down an additional 5½ inches (the width of the joists) to locate the top of the beams. Mark this height.

5 Installing the Beams. As shown in the "Framing Plan," the joists are supported by four long beams and two short beams. Note that the short beams extend 3 inches past the posts on each end. Cut these beams to length. Through-bolt the long beams to the posts with two 3/8x8-inch carriage bolts at each post location. Attach the two short beams to the inside of the posts with two 3/8x3-inch lag screws into each post.

6 Installing the Joists. Measure and cut the square-end rim joists and attach them to the posts with 16d nails. Doubled decking cleats attached to the posts provide nailing for decking and for the

mitered rim joists. Measure and cut the decking cleats with a 45-degree miter on the end of the outer cleats as shown in the drawing. Place the cleats on the short beams and nail them to the posts and the short beam. Measure and cut the mitered rim joists and attach them to the ends

of the square-end rim joists with two 8d nails at each connection.

Measure and cut the three long joists. Place them across the long and short beams. Attach the two outer long joists to the inside of the posts and to the square rim joists with 16d nails. Center the middle long joist between

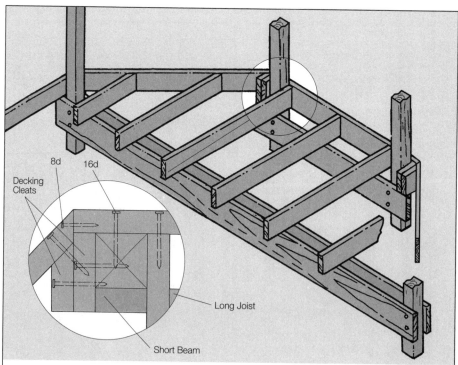

8d   16d

Decking
Cleats

Long Joist

Short Beam

6 Decking cleats provide a nailing surface for the deck boards and the rim joist (inset). Joists are toe-nailed to the beams and face-nailed to the rim joists.

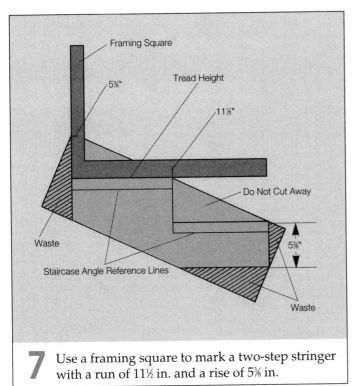

7 Use a framing square to mark a two-step stringer with a run of 11½ in. and a rise of 5⅜ in.

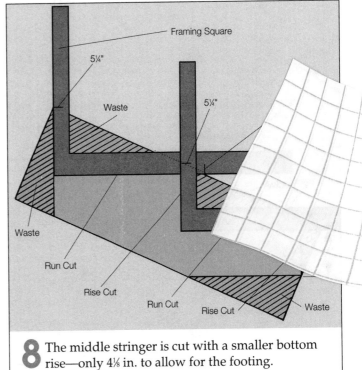

8 The middle stringer is cut with a smaller bottom rise—only 4⅛ in. to allow for the footing.

the first two. Nail this joist to the rim joists. Toe-nail the long joists to the beams with one 8d nail on each side of each connection.

Measure and cut the two short joists with 45-degree miters at each end. Nail the short joists to the posts and to the mitered rim joists. Measure and cut the midlength joists to fit between the mitered rim joists, centered between the short joists and long joists. Nail the mitered ends of the midlength joists to the rim joists and toe-nail them to the long beams.

7 Laying Out the End Stringers. The eight-sided gazebo uses a "housed stringer" design that is identical to the stairs shown in the other gazebos in this book. However, the elegance of the eight-sided gazebo has been enhanced by the addition of stair rails. These rails are optional and you could, in fact, add them to any gazebo in this book.

The stair has a rise of 5⅜ inches and a run of 11½ inches. To make the end stringers, start with two pieces of 2x10, each about 30 inches long. Place a framing square on a stringer as illustrated so that the 5⅜-inch

mark on the outside of the square's tongue and the 11½-inch mark on the outside of the square's blade both align with the top edge of the stringer.

Mark out the rise and the run. Extend the rise line to the bottom of the stringer. You'll cut along this line to make the upper end of the stringer. Now move the square down to lay out the second step, as shown in the drawing. Use the square to lay out the cuts for the front and bottom of the stringers. Measure down 1 inch from the top of the treads and draw layout lines for the stair angles. Lay out the other end stringer.

8 Laying Out the Middle Stringer. You will have to include a middle stringer to support the 32¾-inch-long tread. The middle stringer is designed so that its risers will be recessed 1 inch behind the front of the treads. As you did for the end stringers, use the framing square to lay out the rise and run cuts and the bottom cut. Note that the tongue of the square is now at 5¼ inches for the rise cut while the blade of the square is at 10½ inches for the run cut. Also, the bottom rise cut is 4⅛ inches for the middle

stringer. You can do most of the cutting for the middle stringer with a circular saw. But you'll have to use a handsaw to finish the cuts where rises meet runs so you don't overcut them with the circular saw.

9 Assembling the Stairs. The hardware that connects the treads to the stringers is called a stair angle. Nail the stair angles to the stringers with the nails recommended or provided by the manufacturer. Working with the stringers upside down, nail the stair angles to the bottom of the treads. Each tread is made of two pieces of 5/4x6-inch decking. Cut the treads to 32¾ inches long. Attach the front tread pieces flush to the front of the stringers. Leave 1/2 inch space between the front and back treads. This improves drainage from the steps.

Nail the middle stringer to the front square-end rim joist, centering it between middle front posts. Use two 16d nails driven through the inside face of the beam. Put the stair assembly in place over the middle stringer. Attach it to the front rim joist with framing anchors. Fasten the treads to the middle stringer using two 8d nails at each connection.

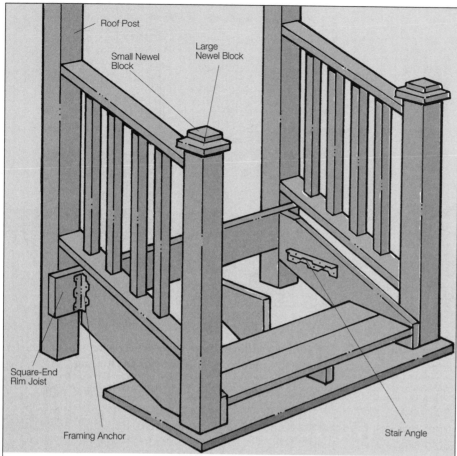

Roof Post

Small Newel Block

Large Newel Block

Square-End Rim Joist

Framing Anchor

Stair Angle

9 Stair angles support the treads on the stringers. Space the two treads 1/2 in. apart.

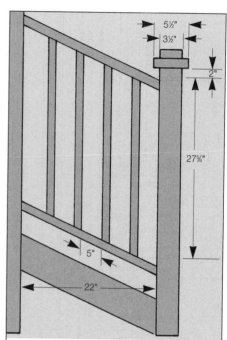

5½"

3½"

2"

27⅝"

5"

22"

10 The front rails attach to the newel posts and the front roof posts. Scribe the angle of the cut on the rail before cutting.

11 Install 5/4x6-inch decking perpendicular to the joists. Use two 8d nails at each joist location.

When the bottom of the stringer sits flat on the concrete slab, the top point of the stringer should extend about 1 inch above the header joist. This is because the calculation for the rise and run of the stair included the 1-inch-thick decking. However, the decking will overhang the header slightly. To allow for this, use a handsaw to cut the top of the stringer flush with the header after you install the stringers.

Cut the two newel posts 41¼ inches long. Attach them to the bottom of the stringers with two 16d nails at each side connection. Nail through the stringers into the posts. Make sure the posts are plumb before you nail.

10 Assembling the Stair Rails. The stair rails will be attached to the two front roof posts. Mark these posts 34¼ inches from the top of the rim joist. This will be the top

of the top rails. Make another mark 5¾ inches from the top of the rim joist. This will be the top of the bottom rails. Now mark where the tops of the rails will meet the rail posts. These marks will be at 10¾ inches from the ground and 2 inches from the top of the post. Theoretically, the rails should be 24¾ inches long with parallel 66-degree cuts on each end. But it's best to scribe these cuts to fit.

Begin by cutting the four stair rails to about 30 inches long. Now align the rails to the marks and scribe the angle cuts at each end. Make these cuts. Screw the rails to the posts with two 3-inch galvanized deck screws at each connection. Screw the small newel block on top of the large newel block with two 3-inch decking screws. Toe-nail the blocks to the newel post top with 8d galvanized finishing nails. Cut the eight 2x2-inch balusters to 27⅝ inches long with 66-degree

angles on each end. Attach the balusters with 3-inch galvanized decking screws through the bottom rails, spacing the balusters 5 inches apart on center, as shown. Toe-screw the balusters into the top rails.

11 Installing the Decking. Install the 5/4x6-inch decking boards perpendicular to the joists using two 8d nails at each joist location. Position the first deck board so that its side overhangs a rim joist by 1/2 inch. Leave it a couple of inches long on each end; you'll trim the deck boards to length after they are all in place. Use the thickness of a 10d nail as a gauge to leave space between the deck boards. When you get within a few boards of the opposite side, check the distance left. You may be able to adjust your spacing slightly to avoid ripping the last board to width. Even if you do have to rip the last board you can make sure it remains wide enough so you can screw or nail it down without splitting.

Snap a line around the perimeter of the deck, leaving the 1/2-inch overhang. If you have a steady eye and hand you can trim the boards using a circular saw without a guide. Otherwise, you can tack a board to the deck to guide the saw. You'll need to cut some of the boards with a handsaw because the posts will get in the way of the power saw.

Framing the Roof

This gazebo uses eight identical curved rafters. It differs from other gazebos in the book in that the roof and posts are tied with ceiling joists. The rafter bird's mouths land on top of the end of the joist.

To lay out the classically graceful rafters you'll use a simple batten bending technique borrowed from boat builders. The curves are easily cut with a saber saw.

1 **Cutting the Posts.** Measure up one post 78 inches from the deck floor. Use a line level to transfer this height to the other posts. Mark and cut the posts to this height.

2 **Installing the Top Plates.** In this gazebo, the top plates and the cap plates are made of 2x6 lumber. As shown in the drawings, the top plates must meet flush to the outside corner of each post. For this

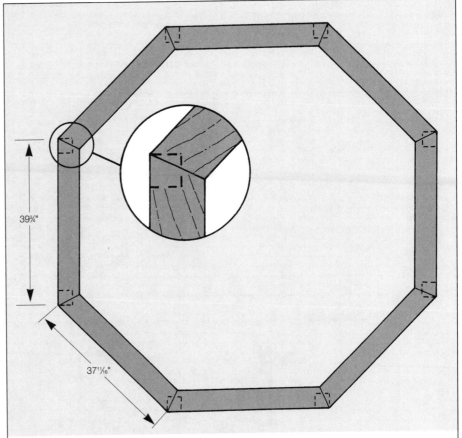

1 Use a line level to mark 78 in. up from the deck floor on each post.

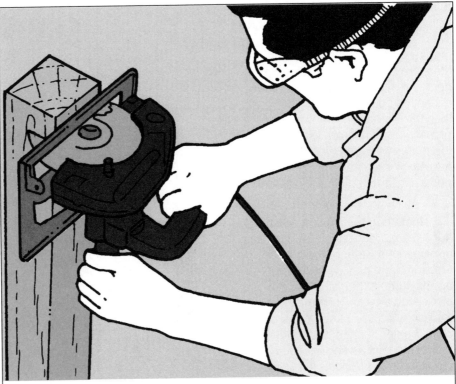

39¾"

37¹¹⁄₁₆"

2 Cut the top plates to meet flush at the outside corner of each post. Nail top plates to the top of the posts.

to happen, the plates must be cut with 67½-degree miters at each end. There will be two alternating plate lengths as shown in the drawing. Measure between the outside corners at the tops of your posts; your distances could be slightly different than the dimensions shown in the drawing and materials list. Cut the top plates with opposing 22½-degree angles on each end to meet over the posts. Nail the top plates to the top of the posts with 16d nails.

3 Installing the Ceiling Joists.
There are two long ceiling joists that span the width of the gazebo. Measure from outside corners of opposing posts to get the length of these two joists. Then make a 1½-inch-wide by 1¾-inch-deep notch in the center of each one so that they form a lap joint as shown. Toe-nail these joists to the posts with 8d nails. Notice in the detail that the joists overhang the faces of the posts slightly. Now measure and cut the short joists with 45-degree bevels on both sides of the ends that meet the long joists. Toe-nail these joists into the long joists and the top plates with 8d nails.

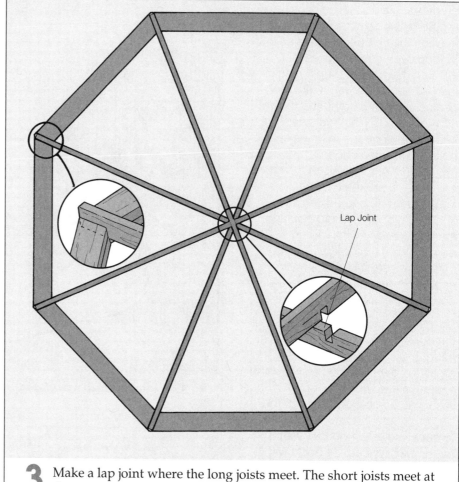

Lap Joint

3 Make a lap joint where the long joists meet. The short joists meet at the center with 45-degree bevels on both sides.

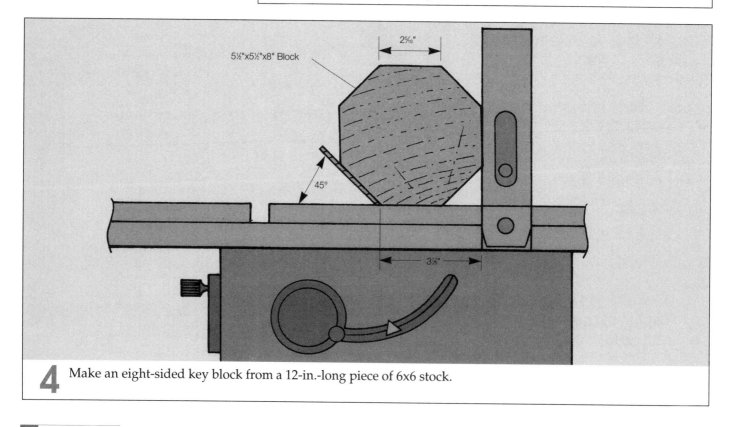

5½"x5½"x8" Block

2⁵⁄₁₆"

45°

3¼"

4 Make an eight-sided key block from a 12-in.-long piece of 6x6 stock.

Measure between the ceiling joists to get the length of the cap plates. Cut opposing 22½-degree miters on both ends of each cap plate. Fasten the cap plates to the top plates with 10d nails. Toe-nail the cap plates to the ceiling joists with 8d nails.

4 **Making the Key Block.** At the peak of the roof, the rafters meet an eight-sided key block made from a 12-inch-long piece of 6x6. Make the block on the table saw. Set the rip fence 3⅞ inches from the blade. Set the blade about 3 inches high and tilt it 45 degrees. Remove the four corners. Cut block to 8 inches.

5 **Making the Pattern Rafter.** The eight curved rafters have a rise of 15 inches per 12 inches of run (refer to the rafter dimensions shown in the drawing). Begin by making a pattern rafter from a 2x8x10-foot-long board. Lay out and cut the bird's mouth and plumb cuts before laying out the curve at the top of the rafter.

To lay out the tail plumb cut, align the 15-inch mark on the framing square blade and the 12-inch mark on the framing square tongue to the top of the rafter as shown. Scribe the tail plumb cut along the blade. Slide the square 12 inches up the rafter to lay out the bird's mouth plumb cut. The bird's mouth seat cut is a 2¾-inch line square to the plumb cut. To lay out the peak cut, place the framing square on the rafter as shown, with the 15-inch mark on the inside of the blade and the 12-inch mark on the inside of the framing square tongue aligned to the bottom of the rafter. Scribe the peak cut on the inside of the blade. Make the cuts.

6 **Cutting the Rafter Curves.** The graceful curves along the top of the rafters are quite easy to make. The secret is to lay them out using a 1/4-inch-thick rip of clear softwood as a bending batten. A strip ripped off a piece of 2-by lumber will work fine, as long as there are no knots.

Drive seven 4d finishing nails halfway into the pattern rafter at the points shown in the drawing. The

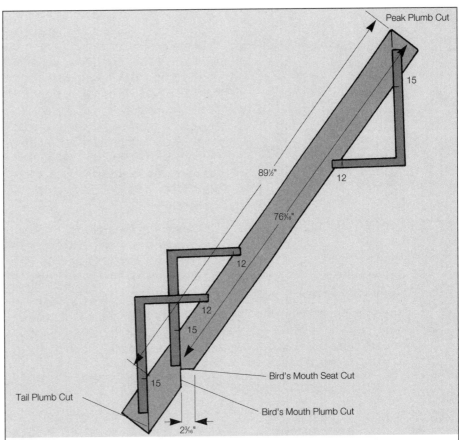

5 Use a framing square in the positions shown to make the peak plumb cut, tail plumb cut, and the bird's mouth cut.

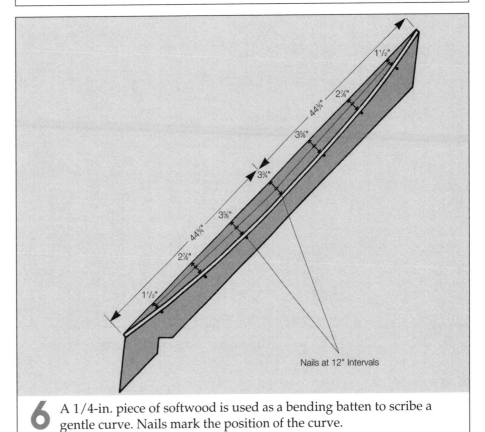

6 A 1/4-in. piece of softwood is used as a bending batten to scribe a gentle curve. Nails mark the position of the curve.

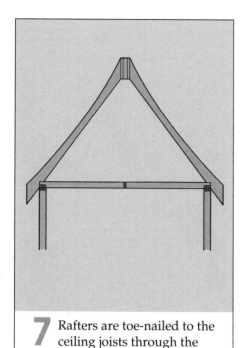

7 Rafters are toe-nailed to the ceiling joists through the bird's mouth cuts. The peak plumb cut is toe-nailed to the key block.

center nail is centered along the top and width of the rafter. All the other nails are spaced at 12-inch intervals. All distances are measured square to the top of the rafter. Bend the batten around the center nail as shown in the drawing. Scribe a line along the length of the batten on the side closest to the top of the rafter. Remove the batten and nails. Cut the curve with a saber saw. Use the pattern rafter to cut the remaining rafters.

7 Installing the Rafters. Toe-nail two rafters to opposing sides of the key block. With a helper, position the assembly on the ceiling joists.

Toe-nail the rafters through their bird's mouths into the top of the ceiling joists with 8d nails. Put the other rafters in position one at a time, toe-nailing them to the key block and joists.

8 Installing the Railings. Like the rim joists, three of the rail assemblies meet the posts squarely and four meet the posts with 45-degree miters. The deck railings are assembled and installed in the same way as the stair railings except for two slight differences: (1) the balusters are cut square at the end and (2) the deck balusters are spaced $5\frac{11}{16}$ inches on center for the square-end rails and $5\frac{3}{8}$ inches on center for the mitered rails.

9 Completing the Roof. Because plywood can't follow the curves of the rafters, the roof is sheathed with 1x4 slats nailed to the rafters with 6d nails. Size the slats for one section of the roof at a time and fit them carefully in place. Cover the slats with 15-lb roofing felt and shingle the roof with composite or wood shingles. Detailed roofing options are given in "Roofing" on page 37.

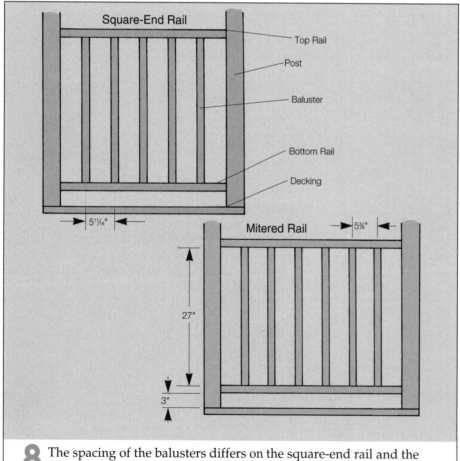

8 The spacing of the balusters differs on the square-end rail and the mitered-end rail.

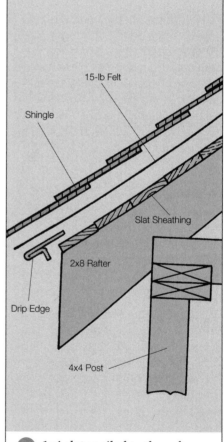

9 1x4 slats nailed to the rafters sheath the roof. Install the slats one section at a time.

Actual Dimensions The exact measurements of a piece of lumber after it has been cut, surfaced, and left to dry. Example: A 2x4's actual dimensions are 1½x3½ inches.

Baluster A vertical railing member that supports the upper and lower rails.

Beam A framing member used to support joists.

Bird's Mouth A notch in a common rafter that fits over the cap plate. It consists of a horizontal cut, called the seat cut, and a vertical plumb cut.

Bull Float A flat metal tool equipped with a long handle used to smooth concrete after screeding.

Cap Plate Horizontal framing member that goes on top of the top plate, tying walls together.

Ceiling Joist Roof framing member that spans the width of a building.

Chalkline String or cord that is covered with colored chalk. It is snapped against a surface to make a mark for cutting or aligning.

Clinching Bending over the exposed tip of a nail, after it has been driven through a board.

Common Rafter A rafter that meets the cap plate with a bird's mouth cut and the ridge or key block with a plumb cut.

Composite Shingles Commonly made of asphalt and fiberglass. They are often made into a three tab strip, which is one of the most popular roofing materials available.

Crook A deviation in a piece of lumber from a flat plane on the narrow face, end to end. A crook makes wood unsuitable for framing.

Decking Boards or plywood nailed to joists to form the deck surface.

Decking Cleats Small pieces that provide support for the decking boards whenever a board ends at a post.

Footing The concrete base that supports posts or steps.

Form Lumber set around the edge to define the shape of the concrete slab.

Frost Heave Shifting or upheaval of the ground due to alternating freezing and thawing of the water in soil.

Gable Roof A roof with two slopes forming triangles on the ends.

Galvanizing Coating a metal with a thin protective layer (e.g., zinc) to prevent rust. Connectors and fasteners should be galvanized for outdoor use.

Grade The ground level. On-grade means at or on the natural ground level.

Hand Edger A hand tool used to round the edges of a concrete slab.

Hip Rafter A rafter that runs diagonally from the ridge to the corners of a building.

Hip Jack Rafters Short rafters that run between the cap plate and a hip rafter.

Joist One in a series of parallel framing members that supports a floor or ceiling load. Joists are supported by beams or bearing walls.

Joist Hanger Metal connectors used to join a joist and a beam so that the tops of both are in the same plane.

Key Block A piece of wood at the peak of a gazebo roof designed to meet the rafters.

Kickback The action that happens when a saw suddenly jumps backward out of the cut.

Lag Screw/ Lag Bolt A large hex-head screw or bolt used to fasten framing members face-to-face; typically used for joining horizontal framing member to posts.

Nominal Dimensions The identifying dimensions of a piece of lumber (e.g., 2x4) which are larger than the actual dimensions (1½x3½).

On-Center A point of reference for measuring. For example, "16 inches on center" means 16 inches from the center of one post, to the center of the next post.

Penny (abbr. d) Unit of nail measurement; e.g., a 10d nail is 3 inches long.

Pitch Number of inches a roof rises per 12 inches of run. Example: A shallow roof would be 4 in 12, while a steeper roof would be 9 in 12.

Plumb Vertically straight, in relation to a horizontally level surface.

Post Anchors Connectors that secure the base of a load-bearing post to a concrete slab or deck.

Ridge The uppermost horizontal line of the roof.

Rim Joist Joist at the perimeter of a structure.

Rise The vertical distance between the cap plate and the peak of a roof.

Run The measure of the horizontal distance over which a rafter rises.

Screeding Using a straight 2x4, moved from one end of a concrete pour to the other, to strike off excess concrete.

Skewing Nails driven into wood at opposing angles to hook the boards together.

Span The horizontal distance covered by a roof.

Square Roofing material is sold by the square; one square is equal to 100 square feet. To determine the number of squares on a roof, measure the area and then divide by 100 (add ten percent to allow for waste).

Stair Angles Clips that support stair treads, eliminating the need for notching the stringers.

Stringer Diagonal boards that support stair treads.

Tacknail To nail one structural member to another temporarily with a minimum of nails.

Tamping Using a rake in concrete work to jab aggregate down and to work out any air bubbles.

Toenail Joining two boards together by nailing at an angle through the end, or toe, of one board into the face of another.

Top Plate Horizontal framing member that forms the top of a wall. In a gazebo, top plates are attached to the top of posts.

Tread The horizontal boards on stairs, supported by the stringer.

Waste Cut The part of the cut that can be used for scrap or thrown away.